QE 2
Cunard's
Flagship

D0539567

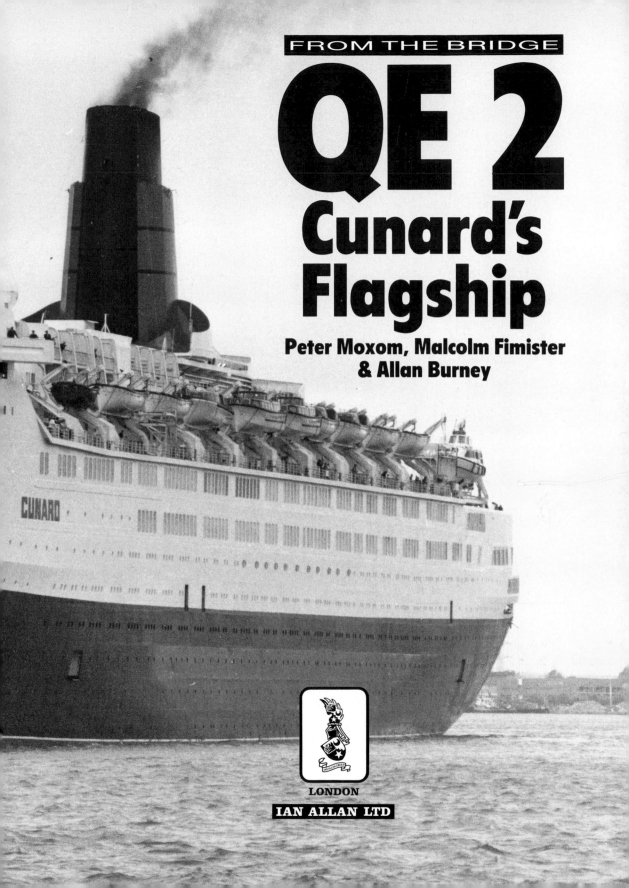

FROM THE BRIDGE

QE 2
Cunard's Flagship

**Peter Moxom, Malcolm Fimister
& Allan Burney**

CUNARD

LONDON
IAN ALLAN LTD

Contents

This book is dedicated to
Capt Alan Bennell

First published 1990

ISBN 0 7110 1876 6

Published by Ian Allan Ltd,
Shepperton, Surrey; and printed
by Ian Allan Printing Ltd at their
works at Coombelands in
Runnymede, England

*All photographs by Allan Burney
unless otherwise credited*

Acknowledgements

With the untimely death of Malcolm Fimister, I
was asked by the publisher Ian Allan Ltd to
complete the manuscript which he had begun to
write. In completing the work I have attempted to
retain as much of the original material as
possible. Without the excellent head-start
afforded to me by Mr Fimister, I doubt if this
book would ever have been completed.

I am also indebted to photographer Allan
Burney who accompanied *QE2* on the voyage
described to New York, and whose superb
photographic contribution has added a dimen-
sion to *From the Bridge: Queen Elizabeth 2*.

Peter Moxom
Stithians, Cornwall 1989

Introduction

The *Queen Elizabeth 2*, flagship of the great House of Cunard and the largest passenger liner in the British Merchant Fleet, emerged from the ashes of a design known at the time as 'Q3'. This embodied a conventional North Atlantic liner of some 75,000 gross tons to replace the ageing *Queen Mary*, to run in tandem with her newer consort the *Queen Elizabeth* and, following the latter's disposal, probably alongside the splendid new *France* by agreement with the French line — Cunard's fiercest rival, but always a respected friend. The year was 1959, at which time the United States Boeing 707 jet airliner, and Britain's smaller de Havilland Comet, had behind them one year of solid entrenchment on their North Atlantic schedules, making increasing inroads in the passenger carryings of the liners — not the least the two *Queens*.

Plans for 'Q3' had reached an advanced stage, and a Government loan towards the massive estimated cost of building the new ship had been agreed before the writing on the wall could be ignored no longer. By 1961, the new breed of jet airliners had increased their stranglehold on transatlantic travel to the extent that losses from the operation of passenger liners had become the rule rather than the exception. To commission a new, conventional giant that was to be reliant (summer and winter) on the North Atlantic passenger trade, possessed every hallmark of disaster. The 'Q3' — however splendid — showed promise of becoming one of the great white elephants of our age! Reluctantly did Sir John Brocklebank, Cunard Chairman at the time, and his Board of Directors, bow to unpalatable facts: the 'Q3' project must be dropped. But what — if anything — to build in her place?

Sir John and his team in Cunard Building, Liverpool, had already focused their thoughts on an entirely fresh design which was promptly dubbed the 'Q4' project. This involved a ship appreciably smaller than 'Q3' in terms of gross tonnage (approximately 58,000), a design that would allow for extensive cruising in the winter months and yet still large and fast enough to provide an adequate running mate for the *Queen Elizabeth* in the shortish summer season on the transatlantic route to and from New York. However, those concerned with the 'Q4' project appreciated that the requirement for a ship of the size envisaged would pose problems, given the need for a service speed of 28½kt and adequate reserves of power, especially as Sir John had emphasised the need to fit twin screws instead of the quadruple arrangement of earlier ships — again mindful of savings in building costs.

At this stage, having become well acquainted with the yard of Vickers at Barrow — which had been the favourite to build 'Q3' — Cunard was able to draw strongly from this yard's experience gained during the design and construction of the magnificent *Oriana* of the Orient Line. Recently completed and now in service, a proven 27½kt had been achieved on a gross tonnage in excess of 40,000. This was a useful starting point, although Cunard must do better.

After tireless research had been expended on drawing boards and in test tanks, the boffins in due time came up with a 58,000-tonner, having a length of 960ft, but a draught of barely 31ft through extensive use of aluminium instead of steel in the superstructure; in the area of propulsion the technical superintendents had opted for a steam turbine plant of Pametrada design fed by just three huge boilers (against the *Queen Mary's* 27). Such would easily provide 28½kt in service, it was claimed, plus ample reserves of power if needed — moreover against greatly reduced fuel consumption. The voracity of the *Queen* ships in this regard had, in later years, contributed significantly to their recurring financial losses.

Subsequently a building contract was signed between Sir John Brocklebank and Lord Aberconway, the Chairman of John Brown & Co, whose famous Clydebank Yard — the traditional builder

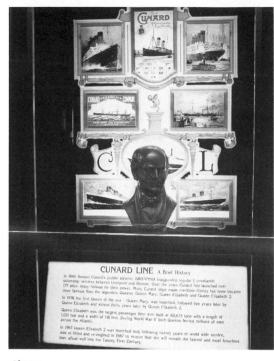

Above:
'Cunard Line: A Brief History' can be found on permanent display onboard at the forward entrance to the No 2 Deck Midships Rotunda.

Above right:
Queen Elizabeth 2 **makes her approach towards the berth of that name at Southampton.**

of great Cunarders — won the order on the basis of an allegedly keener price and earlier delivery. Keel plates were laid in June 1964 and there years later, on a memorable day in September 1967, Her Majesty the Queen launched the ship naming her *Queen Elizabeth 2*, while onlookers on both banks of the narrow Clyde marvelled at the sleek lines and the sparkling white superstructure as the ship dipped gracefully into the restricted tideway. Thereafter the *'QE2'* as inevitably she had become known to the Press and a society of abbreviators, steadily took shape in Brown's fitting-out basin adjoining the slipway. Cunard had engaged an impressive team of décor consultants led by Dennis Lennon, who would ensure collectively that only the best in contemporary taste would be good enough for what was to become Britain's 'shop window' afloat. Exterior styling was the province of John Gardner, who worked in close conjunction with the architectural team to produce the most pleasing possible finish — 'smart, crisp and modern' in the words of Sir Basil Smallpiece, who had by now

replaced Sir John Brocklebank in the Cunard chair. Most controversial of Gardner's work was the ship's single funnel, designed to achieve maximum smoke clearance from the Sports Decks around it. The smoke uptake itself was a tall, black, tapering affair like the crown of an elongated Welsh hat which, by itself, would have looked grotesque but for the stylish shields to either side, which added substance to the structure as a whole. These were painted unrelieved white, the only touches of the famous 'Cunard Red' appearing within the streamlined deflectors at the base of the funnel. Innovative as it might be, the funnel raised a storm of protest from the ship traditionalists — not the least the Cunard Commodore at the time! But given the passage of years, even the funnel's greatest detractors had to concede that it gave *QE2* a character all her own, making her readily identifiable wherever she went.

In December 1968, the great new ship underwent exhaustive speed and other operational trials in the Irish Sea, later to arrive off Greenock Pier a few days before Christmas to embark 500 'guinea pig' passengers. These had been selected from Cunard group shore staff, as well as associates, for the second stage of trials: the testing of hotel services throughout the ship — even to the embarkation and lowering of lifeboats in open ocean. At 28kt the *QE2* proceeded southwards down the Irish Sea, headed for the Canary Islands, her 'guinea pigs' prepared to

Above:
Ever closer! *QE2* **edges in towards her berth, expertly guided by Pilot and tugs.**

enjoy their experience. Alas the new turbines had other ideas! Thanks to a major failure, the ship was reduced to a wallowing 10kt and while it was decided to proceed with the cruise, this became one of 10 days instead of five. When finally she limped into Southampton, for the first time, it was to a deafening silence in place of the blaring sirens that could have been expected had she not been a lame duck.

It was April 1969 before Cunard accepted the ship, and she sailed on her first commercial voyage to New York, following a short shake-down cruise for dignitaries. *QE2* now found herself the flagship of a sadly depleted fleet of but three passenger ships — six of the conventional transatlantic liners, including the *Queens*, having been disposed of since 1965 due to pressing financial problems. The proud new ship traded on, admired wherever she went, but by 1971 the financial state of Cunard had become such that after the customary ritual dance of bid and counter-bid, an offer for its entire share capital was accepted. The buyer was Trafalgar House Investments. This finance house was the original brainchild of a highly effective young property developer who, with the support of two equally effective colleagues, had gained considerable respect in City financial circles for remarkable growth inside their 10 or so years of operation. If there were doubts or fears about the new owners' motives (asset-stripping being the most common theory), these were soon dispelled as Trafalgar

House came to robust grips with its new acquisition and its daunting problems.

Over the years, the *QE2* has had her fair share of difficulty, and the resultant notoricty thanks to an ever-voracious media. Some of these were due to the continuously uncertain temperament of her turbine machinery, which halted the ship and interfered with scheduling in numerous instances. On one occasion, in May 1972, the ship acquired notoriety of a different kind when a squad of Royal Marine Commandos parachuted into a stormy North Atlantic close to the ship, to board her in the hunt for a bomb. A mystery caller to Cunard's New York office alleged an explosive device had been placed aboard, and demanded a ransom of $350,000. The threat turned out to be a hoax for the ransom was never collected at the appointed pick-up location, and the Commandos aboard the liner found nothing despite an exhaustive search.

Fame returned in 1982 when, after adaptation and strengthening of her exterior decks, the *QE2* made a dramatic dash into the South Atlantic, carrying units of the Welsh Guards as reinforcements for the British campaign against the occupying Argentine forces in the Falkland Islands. During her short spell in the Antarctic winter, the ship lay for greater safety off South

Above:
The first line reaches the shore.

earning capacity. Now, following her spell of military service, opportunity was taken to carry out further major refurbishment, for which she was sent back to Lloyd Werft in Bremerhaven, West Germany. At this point the familiar 'Cunard Red' with two black bands was restored to the shields encircling her uptakes, and at the same time the hull was repainted a very light grey. It was said that the Argentinians had dubbed the ship with the nickname of 'Black Slug', which Cunard was anxious to dispel. Whatever the reason for its application, the new livery was not a success because of constant need of re-touching in order to retain her impeccable appearance. At this time the ship was made the subject of one of the 'Whicker's World' programmes on BBC television, and under the scrutiny of the camera her grey hull looked sadly shoddy — especially when viewed in exotic spots like Papeete. Soon she returned to her smart charcoal colouring — known as 'Federal Grey' — contrasting so well with the bright red boot-topping beneath and the dividing white line.

By the early 1980s the cruise industry clearly had become a burgeoning one — particularly in the United States where statistics indicated that little more than a mere 5% of the market had been tapped. Competition began to stiffen annually and the better established operators — intent on retaining their superiority — started to place a string of orders for new ships in Europe and Scandinavia. Moreover, as the cruise boom seemed permanent, an increasing number of newcomers to the scene — bedevilled by one of the worst slumps ever in the international freight market — decided to step in, using some well converted former liners under so-called flags of convenience at sharply competitive fare levels. The purpose-built tonnage appeared, steadily increasing in size (while not always in looks!) alongside the new generation of giant, short-sea ferries commissioning in Europe and Scandinavia. A prominent Norwegian operator even talked of ordering a 200,000-tonner of revolutionary design that seemed to suggest a series of condominia afloat, although at the time of writing this has not reached practical fruition. Nevertheless, it seems that 75,000 gross tons at least will become a standard size for the larger cruise liner, as evidenced by the commissioning of the Norwegian *Sovereign of the Seas*, and the ordering of similar-sized tonnage by the Carnival Cruise Line of Miami.

Georgia which immediately inspired ribald comment from those aboard the P&O *Canberra*, lying in the thick of the combat area, a constant prey to Exocet missiles. Then the *QE2* dashed home with 640 survivors from the frigates *Coventry*, *Antelope* and *Ardent*, receiving a tumultuous welcome on her arrival in Southampton Water.

Throughout her life thus far, during bi-annual drydockings, the ship had been constantly refurbished and upgraded, including the addition of a series of luxury rooms with private verandahs situated on the Sports and Signal Decks between Bridge and funnel — space that had been largely wasted hitherto in terms of

Prominent in cruising as such, but also mindful of the continuing success of its North Atlantic service in summer, Cunard and its Trafalgar parent had to take stock of the future against the rising competition from new or innovatively converted older tonnage. In so many ways was the QE2 still ideal for the role, barring her ageing and troublesome turbine machinery. Following exhaustive technical research and estimated costings, Cunard hit on a characteristically bold idea. It would retain the ship, while removing the existing machinery and replace it with a new diesel-electric system to drive two shafts and a pair of controllable pitch propellers.

This huge, mind-boggling enterprise was undertaken by the celebrated West German yard of Lloyd Werft in Bremerhaven between November 1986 and April 1987 at a cost in the region of £100 million, which also included extensive renovation of, and addition to, the accommodation throughout. Inevitably there were the critics who questioned the wisdom of such monumental expenditure on a near 19-year-old unit, until reminded of the unpalatable cost of a new replacement. Given the excellent condition of her hull, the QE2 should have another 20 years of useful service ahead of her as a result of the conversion, fully measuring up to the standards of new competitors.

When she returned to service in April 1987, the ship experienced the inevitable teething troubles arising from a refit of such magnitude and the use of relatively untried systems. But the fact remains that now she has settled down to her virtually 'new' status, she is as popular as ever. In the words of a prominent commentator on the cruise industry, she is still every inch the great Cunarder — perhaps all the better in looks for her larger funnel — with respect, of course, to Mr Gardner!

This book is about a typical westbound voyage of this great ship from Southampton to New York via Cherbourg, not forgetting some account of the preparation needed for such a trip within the short span of 12hr. It follows the style of Ian Allan's successful 'From the Flightdeck' series in which the reader joins the captain and crew on the Bridge of the QE2 for an inside view of a voyage from Southampton to New York.

Below:
One of the bow tugs eases in under the bow ready to receive her towline so that she can reposition ready for pushing.

Setting the Scene

The *Queen Elizabeth 2* lies alongside at the Southampton terminal of the same name, located on the outer point of the city's famous docks. With 67,000 tonnes of sleek, charcoal-liveried hull and scarlet boot topping, gleaming white upperworks and — soaring above all — a bold new funnel carrying the famous Cunard colours of orange and black, the *QE2* steals the scene on the waterfront.

Thanks to the well established supremacy of the jet airliner, and the near total containerisation of freight, Southampton today is a mere shadow of its former self. The *QE2* now stands alone, whereas 20 years before she would have been but one of a fleet of distinguished liners lying at the docks, disembarking passengers from — or embarking them for — almost every part of the world. As if to emphasise their more recent ousting from the transatlantic routes, the contrails of a big jet pass high above the ship heading for Heathrow.

At a nearby berth lies a Liberian-registered bulk carrier with an unmistakably Greek name, discharging grain to a tall elevator. While alongside the distant Western Docks looms the bulk of a huge container ship, offloading and

Below:
The first visitor is the bunker barge which will replenish the fuel oil used on the previous voyage.

reloading towering tiers of 'boxes', each stuffed with general cargo. Sometimes the *QE2* will have for company the P&O flagship *Canberra*, famous for her own splendid role in the Falklands campaign and now employed exclusively on cruising out of Southampton.

Only the previous afternoon did the *QE2* arrive from New York. Whereas in past years voyage turnrounds were comparatively leisurely affairs, today the economics of operating a ship such as this dictate the shortest possible period between arrival and the disembarkation of passengers, and the subsequent embarkation of 1,800 souls who are taking the new voyage westbound. To

Above:
The aft baggage conveyer is lifted into position on No 2 Deck Aft.

any layman, the idea of achieving this in barely 7hr (overnight stays are rare) is mind-boggling indeed. That the staffs of Cunard — both ashore and aboard — and their Southampton-based Port Agents achieve this, speaks worlds for a thoroughly well oiled system and the dedication of the team as a whole.

Barring unavoidable problems, the fact is that at 22.00hrs this evening, the ship will leave the

berth to make her stately way down Southampton Water at the start of yet another voyage to New York and back, with the added bonus of a short stopover in Cherbourg on the westbound leg. She remains the only passenger liner to operate — albeit for only half the year — the famous transatlantic 'ferry' route of many distinguished predecessors, although even today's passengers will regard the voyage more in the nature of a pleasurable experience than a means of crossing as such. Ironically the QE2 has a staunch ally in the air, for many of her passengers will be returning to England by supersonic Concorde as part of a package deal in conjunction with British Airways, allowing for a few days' stopover in New York. Others — especially the all-important American clientele — will view the voyage either way as an important adjunct to European holidays; others may be businessmen rightly persuading themselves that they need the rest and recuperation afforded by four days aboard

this superb hotel afloat, although the amounts they are likely to eat and drink will do little to improve waistlines without some vigorous daily workout in the ship's 'Golden Door Spa at Sea'.

From the long flagstaff at the ship's stern lazily waves a large Blue Ensign to denote that her Master is currently a member of — or has served in — the Royal Naval Reserve; forward, on a short staff flutters the Cunard pennant with its golden lion rampant clutching the world against a red background. High above the Bridge on the ship's single mast, from one yardarm flies the Blue Peter — officially the international code signal letter 'P' — denoting that the ship is due to sail within the next 24hr; and from the other flies the gold on blue 'Queen's Award to Industry' flag awarded to Cunard for outstanding export achievements. Everybody aboard — whether the Master himself or the professional piano tuner — is united in the single aim to have the ship ready to sail at the appointed time.

The Preparation

The Cunard Line Ltd is the passenger ship division of the Trafalgar House Group of companies. The headquarters of the Cunard Line lie at 555 Fifth Avenue, in midtown New York City, under a resident British chairman. While essentially a British-registered company under overall control from London, it is only logical for what is effectively a worldwide cruise operation to be centred in easily the largest market of the leisure business. This enables full advantage to be taken of the American talent for innovation in terms of fresh ideas and unusual schedules in a swingingly competitive area of business.

Throughout its long history, Cunard has been (certainly in terms of marketing) every inch an Anglo-American operation, and such has been the importance to it of the North American clientele that the company has done little to discourage many Americans from believing that it is an all-out US-owned corporation! The shop window in New York is highly important and there is no secret in the fact that in the golden years of North Atlantic travel, the Cunard offices at 25 Broadway were appreciably more resplendent than even the headquarters at Liverpool or any premises in London.

In South Western House, Southampton, Cunard Line maintains a small team covering Personnel, Medical and Operations Depts. The considerable amount of routine documentation involved in a ship's turnround is today the province of a local agency of long standing in the port.

South Western House itself is an attractive relic of Victorian and Edwardian days, having once been the South Western Hotel, immediately adjoining the platforms of the now defunct Central railway station. Here many passengers would come to pass nights before joining ocean liners with such evocative names as *Mauretania, Aquitania, Berengaria, Majestic, Olympic* and *Leviathan*.

The entrance hall possesses all the erstwhile grandeur of the reception areas of a more splendid era — likewise the main stairways. The rooms — now offices — are of such loftiness that one can barely discern the elaborate friezing of the ceilings, and while today there is, of course, adequate central heating, one senses that it must have been distinctly draughty in those times! Whatever its surroundings, there is nothing Victorian about the Cunard operation here.

The Personnel Dept consists of a small team headed by a UK Manager who reports directly to the Fleet Personnel Manager in New York. They are responsible for the supply, payment and welfare of all Cunard Line Officers and National Union of Seamen (NUS) employed on all of Cunard's seven cruise ships. The majority of the crew aboard QE2 are employed within the Hotel Dept which encompasses Catering, Public Rooms, Accommodation and Cleaning Depts, the employees of the latter being exclusively Filipino. An agency is contracted to supply the manning for the Hotel Dept and this will be explained later and in greater detail.

The Medical Dept is headed by the Company Medical Director who oversees not only the running of the facilities of seven cruise ships, but also of the cargo fleet of quite significant tonnage. He is a medical practitioner of some renown and frequently travels on Cunard Line vessels so as to keep in touch with his 'flock'!

The Operations Dept is headed by the Commodore of Cunard Line, a long-serving expert from the company's Liverpool days. His experience covers just about every ship in the Cunard fleet dating from the immediate postwar era. It fell to him to stand by the QE2 throughout her refit in Bremerhaven, administering the considerable British team that attended this huge operation. Naturally, he is a respected figure in Southampton shipping circles and a member (and past Chairman) of the local Steamship Owners' Association. The Commodore is responsible for the scheduling of each of the seven cruise ships, subject to New York and London's approval, and

Left, top to bottom:
**Storing commences immediately
upon arrival and is invariably
completed minutes before sailing.
The amount and variety of the
stores is awe-inspiring!**

after close scrutiny by all Masters and Navigators concerned on each ship. Scheduling can sometimes run up to 2 years ahead and in any event is finalised at least 12 months in advance.

Storing and replenishment for the Cunard fleet as a whole is overseen by the Assistant VP (Procurement Services) who is in virtual daily contact with the Stores Managers aboard each ship, advising on availability and/or prices of a myriad of goods.

The Stores Manager aboard *QE2* places his order for each port of call some six days in advance, so the supplies arriving today in Southampton will have been telexed ahead from the ship at least a day before arrival at New York on the previous westbound voyage.

A Typical Stores List For a Transatlantic Trip Onboard *QE2*

FOOD

Biscuits	2,000lb
Cereals	800lb
Tinned fish	1,500 tins
Herbs, spices	50lb
Marmalade	9,600 jars
Tea bags	50,000
Coffee	2,000lb
Baby food	600 jars
Caviare	200lb
Butter	3,500lb
Ham	1,200lb
Eggs	30,000
Milk	2,500gal
Lobsters	1,500lb
Grapefruit	3,000lb
Apples	6,000
Lemons	5,000
Grapes	2,000lb
Ice cream	5,000qt
Beef	25,000lb
Pork	4,000lb
Sausages	2,000lb
Ducks	3,000lb
Potatoes	20,000lb
Fresh vegetables	27,000lb
Flour	3,000lb
Rice	3,000lb
Tinned fruit	1,500gal
Jam	300lb
Juices	3,000gal
Tea	5,000lb
Sugar	5,000lb
Dog biscuits	50lb
Foie gras	100lb
Bacon	2,500lb
Cheese	3,000lb
Cream	3,000qt
Fish	8,000lb
Crabmeat	1,000lb
Oranges	15,000
Melons	1,000
Limes	2,000
Frozen fruit	2,600lb
Kosher food	600lb
Lamb	6,500lb
Veal	6,000lb
Chicken	5,000lb
Turkey	5,000lb
Pickles, sauces	2,000 bot

LIQUOR AND TOBACCO

Champagne	1,000 bot
Whisky	1,200 bot
Rum	240 bot
Brandy	240 bot
Sherry	240 bot
Beer	1,200 bot
Cigars	4,000
Tobacco	1,000 tins
Assorted wines	1,200 bot
Gin	600 bot
Vodka	320 bot
Liqueurs	360 bot
Port	120 bot
Beer (draught)	6,000gal
Cigarettes	25,000 pkts

CUTLERY, GLASS AND CROCKERY

Glassware	51,000 items
Kosher crockery	3,640 items
Kitchenware	7,921 items
Crockery	64,000 items
Cutlery	35,850 items
Tableware	64,531 items

LINEN

Tablecloths	5,864
Ovencloths	2,000
Pillow slips	26,200
Bath mats	3,300
Bath towels	26,000
Aprons	3,000
Blankets	8,600
Sheets	23,200
Laundry bags	6,500
Hand towels	31,000
Glass towels	1,400
Deck rugs	1,500

Above:

QE2 has upper deck space for up to two helicopters at any one time. Here can be seen the Trafalgar House helicopter often used to transport VIP guests to and from the ship.

Basically, ships' stores fall into two categories: Food Stores and Dry Stores. Taking food first we have:

● *Meat*

Lamb is invariably purchased and replenished in Southampton, while beef, as could be expected, is bought and replenished in New York – all the better to suit the tastes of American passengers. All meat remains deep-frozen in the ship's refrigerated compartments for use as needed.

● *Poultry*

Again purchasing and replenishment is carried out in the UK with the important exception of turkey, a perennial American taste, which is supplied in New York.

● *Fish*

Most of this is supplied in Southampton and replenished here, and are again deep-frozen aboard the ship until needed.

● *Vegetables*

Replenishment is kept deliberately flexible so as to take advantage of seasonal availability in the UK, France or the US. This applies especially to the more exotic items such as Morels. In this respect, of course, France ranks high as a supplier, and when later in the day the ship touches at Cherbourg, she will obviously take the opportunity to replenish with produce ordered ahead by the Stores Manager aboard.

Wines, spirits and beers also come under the category of Food Stores and the wine list aboard *QE2* is an impressive one, attractively produced in a glossy cover, the inside pages providing maps of the major wine-producing regions in France and Germany. The copious list of red

Below:

Some crew members take a well-earned breather.

Queen Elizabeth 2

Bordeaux wines (Clarets) ranges from a *Chateau Cheval Blanc* at a cool $375 per bottle, to a *Chateau Pape-Clement* for $100, a *Gruard-Larose* at $50 or a *Chateau Millet* at a less bruising $20.

The range of red Burgundies is nearly as comprehensive, while white wines from the French vineyards as well as the Rhine, Mosel, Saar and Ruwer regions of West Germany are also generously featured. For a ship whose predominant customers are American citizens, the excellent wines of California are also prominently listed and have the great advantage of bearing more modest prices. For the post-prandial drinker there is a full range of Cognacs, liqueurs and Port wine supplied by the best Oporto shippers. All wines – even those from California – are purchased and replenished in Southampton.

Still on the subject of drink, about 90% of spirits are purchased in the UK, with the obvious exception of Bourbon whisky. Of the 'Scotch' variety, there are few brands that are not available in the ship, although American passengers currently seem to hold a preference for three or four particular marks.

Beers are predominantly UK-supplied with the exception of American household names such as Budweiser. For the consumption of passengers and crew alike, draught beer is supplied in bulk by Courage's road tankers and pumped into a tank aboard of 12,000gal capacity.

Still within the category of Food Stores, we have the more exotic delicacies, the obvious one being caviar. Only the best Russian grades such as Beluga or Malossol are purchased on a quantity basis of eight tons per year and spread across the seven ships of the Cunard passenger fleet, the *QE2* being the heaviest consumer for her size and capacity. *Pâté de Foie Gras* – with or without truffle – is consumed at an average of about 1,000 tins per voyage, purchased and replenished at Southampton, while another popular delicacy – Scotch smoked salmon – disappears at the rate of half-a-ton on every voyage! Americans especially have a strong appetite for strawberries, even eating them for breakfast. On embarkation, passengers are welcomed to their rooms by a dish of the fruit accompanied by a half-bottle of the Cunard-Ritz house Champagne produced by the vineyard of De la Haye – a nice complimentary touch! Needless to say that there is a wide range of Champagnes offered on the wine list – *Bollinger, Veuve Cliquot, Moet & Chandon, Dom Perignon* and *Mumm Cordon Rouge* to name but a few.

Right:
Onboard Stores Manager Erich Graf inspects the famous *QE2* wine cellar.

So much for the principal Food Stores under constant replenishment at Southampton. Now we turn to the very broad area of Dry Stores, stretching from technical items to all kinds of cutlery, glassware and china, and from notepaper to printed material:

● *Furniture and Furnishings*
Here the carpeting is entirely of UK manufacture, supplied and replenished at Southampton, while 95% of the furniture and other materials are also of British source and replenished on this side as required.

● *Paint*
For the charcoal-coloured hull, the red boot-topping and the towering white upperworks – not to mention all other painted areas – paint is also British-supplied under contract. Invariably in pristine order, the *QE2* constantly requires retouching in all parts.

● *Crockery*
In the Columbia and Mauretania Restaurants, the crockery is of Royal Doulton bone china attractively stamped with the Cunard lion-rampant – in this case gold-lined. Inevitably the breakage rate is high and replacements are placed aboard at each turnround in Southampton.

● *Cutlery*
Here again the principal restaurants and grill rooms are equipped with a high standard of cutlery – all silver-plated. Some of the larger items even date from famous predecessors such as the old *Queen* liners and others. During the

Above:
A small portion of the many hundreds of floral arrangements delivered onboard at every embarkation port.

recent refit, no less than 400,000 of these prize pieces were resilvered, including meat trolleys each with a silver-plated dome. There are also 150 Flambé burners, still fuelled by methylated spirits, which is carried aboard the ship under the strictest control, on the insistence of the Department of Transport surveyors.

Below:
Seven Deck Dry Stores: the largest grocer's shop in the world!

Left:
The piano tuner is hard at work in the Midships Rotunda on No 2 Deck.

Each provides a professional arranger and both are busy ladies – not only during turnround, but also the voyage itself, for there is nothing more suggestive of shoddiness than tired flowers!

● *Printed Material*

For example, ship's notepaper and menu covers for every conceivable type of celebration are also supplied at Southampton, along with the daily programme sheets and invitation cards for the Officers' cocktail parties. Stocks of Immigration and Customs forms are also carried for circulation among all passengers.

● *Ship's Uniforms and Working Rig*

This is another important area – nowadays, coming under the direct control of the Chief Officer. In a ship of this calibre, smartness at all times is essential.

● *Pianos*

During turnround every piano in the ship must be checked and carefully tuned for use by the professionals during the voyage. Thus, in every room where there is a piano, one sees professional tuners – oblivious to the hubbub around them. Pianos can be special sufferers from bad weather conditions and consequent heavy movement of the ship, necessitating repair, or even replacement on occasion during turnround. All these items are but representative of the vast variety of equipment delivered into the ship for each voyage.

● *Glassware*

Here again the breakage rate is high but nevertheless the glass is of good quality crystal – all replaced at Southampton as needed.

● *Hospital and Medical Supplies*

In this vital area, Cunard uses the services of consultants for advice on the medicines and drugs in constant need by the ship's hospital, or for dispensing aboard on the prescription of either of the two Medical Officers. Needless to say, a wide range needs to be available for a variety of maladies.

● *Floral Decoration*

There are two contractors employed – one for cut flowers and the other for large floral arrangements in the public rooms and areas of the ship.

As many as 2-300 boxes and cartons delivered to the ship contain what are termed as Technical Stores, and these are handled by the onboard dept of that name. Anything from batteries to spanners, safety boots to screws, all are stored onboard for immediate use at any time by any dept. The range and variety of Technical Stores has grown so much that one of the six cargo holds within the ship had to be taken over as a stockroom. This has dramatically reduced QE2's car-carrying capabilities and with the introduction of grinding and storage facilities for garbage in No 6 Hold there remains just No 5 Cargo Hold for the carriage of motor cars – and some are very prestigious indeed. Now QE2 can carry perhaps only 12 motor cars as opposed to 30 plus not so long ago.

The Junior Second Officer is traditionally delegated as Cargo Officer and on many in-port days he could be found behind the wheel of a luxury sports car imagining himself winning at

Left:
Just one small section of the labyrinthian Technical Storeroom.

Above:
QE2's car-carrying capabilities are not just limited to sports cars and limousines: here, two vintage cars arrive for onloading for New York.

Left:
Time in port is never wasted: First Officer Peter Moxom gets to grips with the latest delivery of Admiralty Chart Corrections (for the 'eagle-eyed', the Combinator levers are showing an ahead pitch owing to routine tests being carried out in the ECR).

Le Mans, or perhaps cruising the 'Strip' with the hood down. His dreams are frequently shattered when the back end of his 'chariot' is suddenly lifted vertically and laterally by six beefy dockers who are trying to shunt 7ft of car into a 6ft space. When they discover that seven into six will not go without little fractions to worry about, their language becomes fairly colourful. When they discover that behind the tinted glass of this millionaire's toy there sits 180lb of budding rally driver they positively rage, and Junior Second Officer rapidly learns that crossing a field of raging bulls is probably far more preferable than crossing the path of half-a-dozen 18st dock-workers.

Safety

Any description of the voyage preparation processes would be incomplete without reference to the vital aspect of safety of life at sea and the continuous vetting of all safety equipment by Government and other officialdom. A vessel the size of QE2 cannot, for every practical reason be surveyed from bow to stern at one single attempt.

There are two official bodies concerned: HM Government's Department of Transport (DoT) surveyors and Lloyd's Register of Shipping, who between them co-operate to divide the hull, machinery and equipment into a number of areas for survey. The former is responsible for issuing the statutory annual passenger certificate, while Lloyd's Register is responsible for classification of the ship for insurance purposes.

Above:
A £¼ million worth of hi-tech garbage-grinding machinery.

As much as possible of the hull and machinery survey is carried out by Lloyd's surveyors during the *QE2's* bi-annual drydocking when she is withdrawn from service for a minimum period of 10 days. However, in the intervening year, statutory inspection of the hull surfaces under-water is carried out by divers equipped with waterproof cameras, acting on the instructions of surveyors watching a television screen from a boat on the surface. Scrutiny by this means is every bit as effective as that by the naked eye – indeed possibly more so since there is nothing the camera misses, especially on enlargement of the negative.

Because of the magnitude of their task, it follows that the work of the DoT surveyors, covering every aspect of safety at sea, becomes a continuous process, involving a surveyor's visit to the ship at practically every turnround. One may thus draw a parallel with painting the Forth Bridge, for no sooner have surveyors completed their cycle of work at the stern of the ship than it is time to start at the bow!

During a typical turnround at Southampton, DoT surveyors will attend aboard the ship immediately on her arrival to call on the offices of the Chief Engineer or the Chief Officer (or both) in response to an earlier telexed call from either. At this particular turnround the Chief Engineer's area involves a pump, ready stripped for examination under the continuing cycle, as well as a remotely controlled valve system for checking. The Chief may also take the oppor-tunity to discuss a slight problem area such as may have arisen with the Reverse Osmosis installation, the latest and most sophisticated method for producing fresh water from salt. This system consists of 12 banks of membranes through which sea water is forced at a pressure of 750lb/sq in (50 Bar), resulting in all solids being retained by the system and pure, clean fresh water being produced at a rate of 500 tonnes every 24hr.

Again today, the deck department of the Chief Officer involves inspection of one of the water ballast tanks, which has been drained and ventilated, in preparation for inspection. In this case the tank is filled with water to the top of an overflow pipe on deck and the surveyor will crawl over every part of the tank casing to see how the steelwork stands up to the water pressure exerted from within – a process known as 'Pressing Up'. He will also satisfy himself that the tank is being subjected to maximum pressure by observing the rate of flow from the overflow pipe, or by visiting the Safety Control Room on No 2 Deck, where there are pressure gauges for every fluid tank throughout the ship.

On another occasion one of the fuel tanks will have been emptied and ventilated sufficiently for certifying by a chemist as safe for entry. The surveyor will clamber inside the tank itself to examine its internal condition, as well as the filling and draining pipes. Responsibility for the condition of the tanks is delegated by the Chief Officer to his Senior First Officer as the Tank Commander, earning for himself the nickname of 'Rommel' – reminiscent of the famous German Panzer commander of World War 2. Rommel will accompany the surveyor in his thankless task and a further officer will stand by the tank entrance to listen, render assistance or raise the alarm if necessary.

While not a feature of today's turnround, the vital system for operating the fire-resistant doors and fire valves for ensuring complete sub-division and the prevention of spreading, requires regular checking.

On still other occasions a fire drill may be planned by the Captain and the Chief Officer in virtual secrecy so that foreknowledge of the location of the mock fire exercise will be unavailable to the firefighting parties. Prior to the alarms being sounded an announcement is made over the public address system to alert all staff and passengers. Such drills are made as realistic as possible even to the provision of some innocuous smoke in the exercise area – for instance the aft steering compartment. Not only must the teams demonstrate practical firefighting skills, but also individuals wearing breathing apparatus are required to rescue dummy victims lying prone in the smoke-filled compartment.

Periodically a surveyor will require to witness the carrying out of a full-scale boat drill, or may attend an unofficial drill of this type. Key personnel are required to muster at their Boat or Raft Stations, wearing lifejackets, following which a number of lifeboats on the outboard side of the ship will be turned out of their davits and with correct lowering procedures being followed will allow the boat to 'fall' to the water. The boat crew will then give each boat a brief run clear of the ship before returning to their respective falls for recovery to the Boat Deck.

These are but a few examples of the vigilance which is applied constantly to safety. The surveyors are strict because they have to be, and during their perambulations around the ship they keep a practised eye lifted for any sign of deficiency, which is rarely found. It is important psychologically that all shipboard staff know that they are under the constant surveillance of Inspectors and Officers alike and the relationships maintained under this umbrella are ones of mutual respect and friendly co-operation.

Joining the Ship

Whereas in the heyday of North Atlantic sea travel, there were usually two boat trains to transport passengers from London's Waterloo station directly to the ship's side in the Southampton terminals, today there is but one. In the golden years of transatlantic voyaging, the boat train was reckoned to be the smart way to join the ship and the Southern Railway rose to the occasion in every respect. The train was a veritable mini Orient Express as aristocrats, famous film stars of both sexes and industrial tycoons puffing at outsize Havana cigars, mingled on grimy platforms, which for a short while became centres of high society, press bulbs flashing on all sides. Often ladies would be accompanied by pets — pekingese and poodles as elaborately coiffed as their mistresses, one young Hollywood raver even turning up with a pet baby leopard which was rather too playful for the comfort of her fellow passengers.

Shortly the passengers would be persuaded to take their seats in elegant brown and gold Pullman coaches, at linen-clothed tables each with its lamp and red shade. Slowly the train would pull out, leaving the platform to descend from its heady half-hour in the limelight until the next time, probably the following day — such was the frequency of sailings between Cunard and its competitors.

Today all is changed: for one thing there is only one train; for another no longer is it the popular method of joining the ship. For this particular sailing the boat train will be bringing but 400 passengers to the ship out of the 1,800 or so booked, the majority arriving now by a combination of private cars, limousines, scheduled

Below:
A boat train lies alongside the *Queen Elizabeth 2* Terminal at Southampton Docks.

train services and then taxis to carry them to the terminal, or long-distance coaches — especially those booked as special groups by the tour operators or prize promoters. For today's 22.00-hrs departure, the boat train is scheduled to leave Waterloo at 15.20hrs to arrive in the terminal at 16.24hrs, embarkation as a whole beginning at 16.00hrs.

The boat train pulls into the *Queen Elizabeth 2* terminal only two or three minutes behind schedule and its passengers now alight, all but their hand baggage being taken by porters for stacking at the entrances adjacent to the

gangways and for X-ray screening, before being loaded aboard for distribution throughout the ship according to the cabin numbers written on the labels.

Meanwhile, from the train on the lower level of the terminal, passengers have been directed to escalators that carry them to the large check-in hall above, where there are 22 desks and attendant staff for the checking of tickets, passports and US visas. Once past the desks, they proceed directly to the security point for examination of their hand luggage and personal screening through the type of gate in use at airport terminals.

Plan of Southampton Docks showing (bottom right) the *Queen Elizabeth 2* Terminal and position of the ship itself before and after unberthing

Following security, passengers walk the few paces to the Immigration desks to have their passports checked for validity, after which those foreigners who have purchased goods in England and are proceeding home, will have the relevant invoices stamped by Customs for reclamation of Value Added Tax. With these relatively painless procedures behind them, passengers may proceed to embarkation across either of two gangways to the ship — one amidships leading to the main lobby, and one further aft on No 2 Deck. As likely as not, one of the ship's photographers, with camera at the ready, will take a 'happy snap' to record their arrival aboard — a picture that will be displayed later in the voyage on a board among hundreds of others. Soon they have stepped through the ship's shell door to be directed to their rooms. For them the voyage has begun!

No description of the departure preparation would be complete without comment on the work of the Port Agents for Cunard, who attend to all the documentation that accompanies a ship's arrival and departure. The agency is one of long standing and experience — a thoroughly respected name on the waterfront which at one time represented the famous French Line and others in Southampton. Approximately one week in advance of the QE2's arrival, the Agents will have given provisional notice of this to the Port Authority (in this case Associated British Ports), as well as requesting Customs attendance on the appropriate form — one for weekdays and the other for a Sunday arrival. From HM Customs and Excise, the requisite storing authority will also be obtained at this point for spirits and tobacco goods. Then, about three days from the ship's arrival, final notice will be tendered, giving a detailed description of the proposed working arrangements. At the same time, application to the Port Authority for the provision of shore cranes on the quayside by the terminal is made. On arrival of the ship, she is promptly 'Entered in and Out' with Customs, and the Master's C13 Form is also submitted, as well as a declaration of any goods carried on the open deck of the vessel.

Following the departure of the ship, the Agents must report her passenger carryings to Customs both on arrival and departure, for which there is again a specific form to complete. Beyond this there is the important ordering of tugs in advance from the two contractors used in Southampton, the Alexandra Towing Co — a celebrated operation with its headquarters in Liverpool, having followed Cunard's big ships to Southampton when their base was shifted south — as well as Red Funnel Steamers, perhaps better known to holidaymakers as principal operators

of the Isle of Wight ferry service for many years. These two companies share the Cunard work between them. Pilots must also be ordered for both arrival and departure and, finally, after the ship has left, the Agents must confirm her arrival/departure to the Port Authority for its records.

Much of this agency work is routine, but preparation of the requisite documentation is long and painstaking, besides which the Managing Director of the agency company on turnround days satisfies himself constantly that 'all systems go', covering a considerable mileage on his feet in this process!

These then are but a few of the principal areas of activity during turnround at Southampton, and thanks to the exigent effort of the entire team, QE2 is ready to sail by 21.30hrs on a scheduled departure time of 22.00hrs.

Below:
Southampton Docks at night, photographed from the QE2's port Bridge wing.

Departure

It is now 21.35hrs with departure scheduled for 22.00hrs. In his capacious office, or day-room, the Master of the ship sits at his desk, attending to a mound of paperwork requiring his attention. The door to the office remains open, a railed curtain drawn across it. There is a knock on the open door and the face of the Southampton Pilot appears around the curtain. While very easily could he have proceeded directly to the Bridge, letting one of the Junior Officers report his presence, the Pilot elects to make his number with the Master out of respect, without expecting to linger, for there should be nothing unusual about today's departure.

'Hallo Dan', the Master greets this old friend, 'I'll be with you shortly.' With that the Pilot turns to walk along the alleyway leading to the staircase to the Wheelhouse directly above. For a few minutes more the Master concentrates on his administrative work until at 21.45hrs there comes another knock on the door to reveal the

Below:
Preparation for departure: Second Officer Ian McNaught attempts to unravel the mysteries of push-button dialling while Coxswain Stuart Daw runs through a final check of the steering systems.

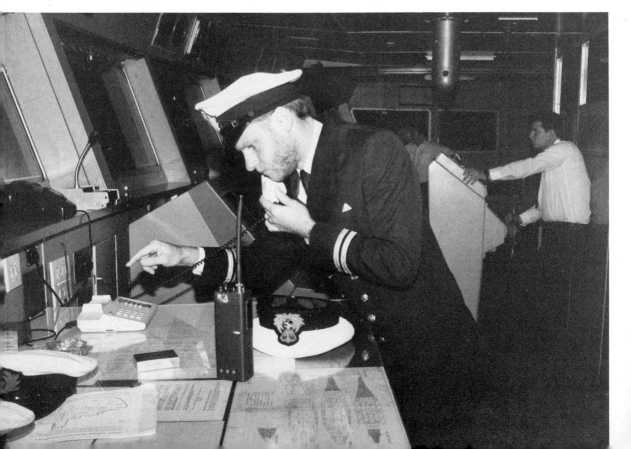

Left:

First Officer Peter Moxom checks with the Electronics Engineers that all is ready with the 'Sailing Music', broadcast over the open decks during departures . . .

Above:

. . . and notifies the Captain that all is ready for departure.

Form FRE 13

DRAUGHT OF WATER AND FREEBOARD
NOTICE

Issued by the Department of Trade pursuant to Section 10 (2) of the Merchant Shipping (Load Lines) Act 1967

SHIP .... PORT OF REGISTRY ....

GROSS TONNAGE ....
(Where a ship has alternative gross tonnages, both must be given)

(1) Summer freeboard * .... millimetres corresponding to a mean draught † of.................................... millimetres (equal to .... feet .... inches).

(2) Winter freeboard * .... millimetres corresponding to a mean draught † of.................................... millimetres (equal to .... feet .... inches).

(3) Tropical freeboard* .... millimetres corresponding to a mean draught † of.................................... millimetres (equal to .... feet .... inches).

(4) Winter North Atlantic freeboard* .... millimetres corresponding to a mean draught † of .... millimetres
  (equal to .... feet .... inches).

(5) Allowance for fresh water for all freeboards other than timber freeboards* .... millimetres .

(6) Timber Summer freeboard* .... millimetres corresponding to a mean draught † of .... millimetres (equal to .... feet .... inches).

(7) Timber Winter freeboard* .... millimetres corresponding to a mean draught † of .... millimetres (equal to .... feet .... inches).

(8) Timber Tropical freeboard* .... millimetres corresponding to a mean draught † of .... millimetres (equal to .... feet .... inches).

(9) Timber Winter North Atlantic freeboard* .... millimetres corresponding to a mean draught †'of .... millimetres
  (equal to .... feet .... inches).

(10) Allowance for fresh water for timber freeboards* .... millimetres.

* Particulars to be given above of freeboards and allowance for fresh water are to be taken from the load line certificate currently in force in respect of the ship. Paragraphs referring to freeboards which the certificate shows have not been assigned to the ship must be deleted.

† The mean draught to be given above is the mean of the draughts which would be shown on the scales of measurement on the stem and on the stern post of the ship if it were so loaded that the upper edge of the load line on each side of the ship appropriate to the particular freeboard were on the surface of the water.
  Where the draught is shown on the scales of measurement on the stem and on the stern post of the ship in feet the mean draught must be given in both millimetres and feet and inches using an equivalent of 25.4 millimetres to one inch.

		PARTICULARS OF LOADING						
1	2	3	4	5	6	7	8	9
		ACTUAL DRAUGHT			MEAN FREEBOARD		SIGNATURE OF MASTER AND AN OFFICER	
Date	Place	Forward	Aft	Mean	Actual (see notes 1 and 2 below)	Corrected (see note 3 below)	Master	An Officer

Above:
Capt Alan Bennell and Senior Pilot Dan Robson discuss the tide situation.

- One of the three First Officers whose Watch it is.
- One of the three Second Officers whose Watch it is.
- The Coxswain on the wheel, a seaman Petty Officer.
- An additional Coxswain in case of need.
- A boy seaman to assist generally.

Last but not least in this tight little team is the Southampton Port Pilot, one of two appropriated by the Cunard Line (though not exclusively, of course). Both are highly skilled in their art, and most probably each has handled the *QE2* more times than he can count on either arrival or departure. Invariably, nevertheless, the Master retains the overriding responsibility for his ship and may, if he considers fit, assume control at any moment, although such situations are virtually unheard of, given pilots of such calibre as this pair. All commands, whether by Master or Pilot, are directed to the First Officer on Watch, who redirects them to the appropriate station by means of his 'walkie-talkie' radio telephone handset on a particular frequency, to which the other stations, each with its own handset, is tuned.

The Pilot has his own handset but tuned to a different frequency, since through it he will be controlling every movement of the attendant tugs, addressing each by its name in the process.

It is vital that the Master himself should remain free of involvement in the relaying of orders in the interests of keeping a clear head and a wary eye on the departure procedures as a whole. Clearly, the First Officer on Watch will stay close to Master and Pilot to ensure that no command is missed, as will the Staff Captain in his capacity as Deputy Master.

We now move forward to the open deck immediately above the bow of the ship where another of the First Officers directs the mooring party. With him are two of the ship's carpenters (popularly known as 'chippies') of Petty Officer rank, who are responsible for the massive, electrically operated anchor capstans, ensuring that the two anchors are functional at all times. Although not in use at present, they must be available instantly to let go in the event of a sudden emergency.

The mooring party itself is actually located one deck beneath the First Officer, within the hull of the ship. This was a deliberate design to avoid cluttering the foredeck with mooring equipment other than the anchor capstans (cable lifters) and anchor cables, although it means that the Petty Officer in charge (invariably the Bo'sun) is virtually sightless (the actual mooring lines

First Officer on Watch, a key member of the Bridge party on departure.

'All on schedule for 22.00 departure sir', he reports.

'Thank you Peter. I'll be up in five minutes', the Master replies.

Meanwhile, as soon as the Pilot has reached the Bridge, the Coxswain records 'Pilot — Mr Robson on Bridge 21.45hrs' in the Bridge Movement Book, an official written record of everything that happens during arrivals and/or departures.

Back in his office, the Master glances at his wall clock, rising to pick up his hat, straighten his jacket and leave the room, heading for the Wheelhouse stairway.

Before describing the departure procedures in some detail, we should first identify the deck parties that constitute Departure Stations at key points in the ship. Firstly, and most importantly, is the Bridge itself from which all control of the ship's manoeuvres is exercised. Here we see:
- The Master of the ship (Master being essentially his function and Captain his title).
- The Staff Captain (ranking second in seniority and present in case the Master is taken ill and he must assume immediate command).

Left:
'The Driving Force' – from left to right: Staff Capt Ron Bolton (Communications, Bow Thrusters and Steering), First Officer Peter Moxom (Combinators), Capt Alan Bennell (Overall Command) and Pilot Dan Robson.
(Caps are often removed if weather conditions dictate, owing to the exposed position of the Bridge wing consoles.)

Above:
The Pilot advises Southampton Port Radio of our imminent departure from the berth.

passing through narrow fairleads in the shell plating either side of the bow), and must rely on the talkback system or walkie-talkie for receiving the First Officer's commands.

Moving aft to the gangway parties, we find the Chief Officer responsible for the closing of all the watertight shell doors through the ship's side, once the gangways have been landed. Remembering a recent ferry disaster, this precaution is of vital importance — although in the ferry's case the action was all the more crucial since the doors were at the bow of the ship, squarely in the way of the bow wave which increased in size as the ship gathered way.

On the Bridge the Second Officer of the Watch has completed the lengthy list of sailing announcements and is now in the process of closing all internal watertight doors so as to fully comply with the latest DoT Regulations.

Finally the Aft Mooring Station is the responsibility of one of the off-Watch Second Officers, although unlike the Forward Party it has the slight advantage of working on a deck open to the sides so as to afford virtually all-round vision.

The *QE2* lies with her port side to the quay, heading downstream, and now the Master joins

the Pilot, Staff Captain and the First Officer of the Watch on the port Bridge wing where they enjoy uninterrupted views overside, forward and aft. In the wheelhouse itself stand the Duty Second Officer, the Coxswain at the wheel — set directly behind the long control console — the standby Coxswain and the Duty Deck Boy.

At this point the Master gives his approval for the unmooring procedure to start:

- Tugs are made fast fore and aft as requested.
- Vessel should already be at 'Ready To Sail Mode' which means that a minimum of four engines are up and running on line with the propeller shafts stationary.
- 'Go Independent Fore and Aft', whereby all moorings are singled-up fore and aft so that upon the command 'Let Go', all ropes and wires could be recovered simultaneously on independent winches.
- The aft wire spring is let go and recovered aboard. Upon the report being received on the Bridge that the aft wire spring is gone and clear, the propeller shafts can then be rotated.
- 'Combinator Mode' is selected on the Wheelhouse console after first advising the ECR (Engine Control Room) that this is required. The propulsion motors then receive power from the four or five main engine alternators and the propellers commence turning at 72rpm on zero pitch. This is all a new necessity since the Bremerhaven refit in 1986-87. With 9 × 9-cylinder MAN/B&W turbocharged marine diesel engines producing 10.5MW of electrical power each to two GEC 40MW electric propulsion motors, *QE2* now boasts the most powerful diesel-electric plant afloat.

If the onlooker might now be expecting a scene of drama and the repeated bellowing of orders on all sides, he will certainly be disappointed. In fact there is no more than a prevailing air of vigilant informality about the Bridge team as it moves quietly through a well-practised drill in swift sequence — so swift as to make the constant string of commands through the walkie-talkie nearly simultaneous and difficult to follow. It is two minutes to 22.00hrs:

- The Chief Officer reports that the last gangway into the ship has been landed ashore
- The Master orders 'Let go all wires', by which all mooring wires forward and aft are slacked down from the ship and released from the bollards ashore by the shore gangs, and quickly recovered aboard

There are four tugs in attendance — two made fast forward (one on each bow) and two made fast aft (one on each quarter) — to take the ship off the quay. Through his walkie-talkie the Pilot has already positioned them according to the power capability of each.

All is now poised for unberthing. With nodded assent or an 'Off we go then' from the Pilot, the Master orders 'Let go everything' and all remaining mooring lines (ropes) fore and aft are released. Non-mariners, and in fact experienced seamen, occasionally are unaware that regardless of size, age or employ, a ship has only one 'rope' aboard her, that being the ship's bell rope — all other so-called ropes being either 'lines', 'sheets' or 'halliards'!

Engines and rudder are now to the Pilot's orders — in the popular Navy term 'he has the con'!

As the last line leaves the quay the Duty Second Officer within the Wheelhouse switches off the aft-facing forward decklights so as to afford night vision to the Bridge team and switches on the navigation lights. These are, as the law requires, two white masthead lights one abaft of and higher than the other. A white light facing aft (sternlight), a green light (sidelight) to starboard and a red to port.

Much has been published over the years as to the myth and legend surrounding the origin of the terms starboard and port, but little if any has been mentioned about the origin of the term 'Bridge'. It is this author's belief that the term originated many years ago when sailing vessels had small raised 'castles' built on either side of their aft decks to improve their range of visibility. Each 'castle' was fitted with a ship's wheel so that depending on which tack the vessel was on she could always be steered from the high (windward) side. To ensure a rapid transit between steering positions when tacking (changing course) a bridge was made between the castles — probably from planks of timber. Over the years this has become 'the Bridge' — the position from which the vessel is steered.

By now the forward and aft mooring parties have recovered their lines and very soon both report 'All clear forward' and 'All clear aft' respectively. The Bridge control levers, regulating propeller pitch, are now manipulated by the Duty First Officer to the Pilot's direction. In the *QE2*, and others today, all vestige of conventional orders to the engine room has vanished into history, giving way to commands in terms of Pitch Ahead or Astern issued electronically by way of the control levers to receivers far below in the machinery spaces. One might imagine that this would involve getting used to, but both Pilot and Officers seem to have assimilated the new system to the manner born.

The Pilot has, by this time, instructed all four tugs to pull on previously instructed headings. All are now at full ahead, their wires leading up to the ship tighter than piano wires, the water boiling under their sterns. By a combination of tugs, Bow Thruster and main propellers the Pilot eases the ship off the quay, ever wary of the unpredictable current eddies that plague this section of Southampton Water and ready to counter any ambition the ship may have to 'sail away' as the wind acts on the huge area of 'windage' created by a vast hull area and massive funnel.

The ship channel lies some 300yd to starboard and it is the Pilot's aim to have the bow lined up as nearly as possible therein to proceed down-

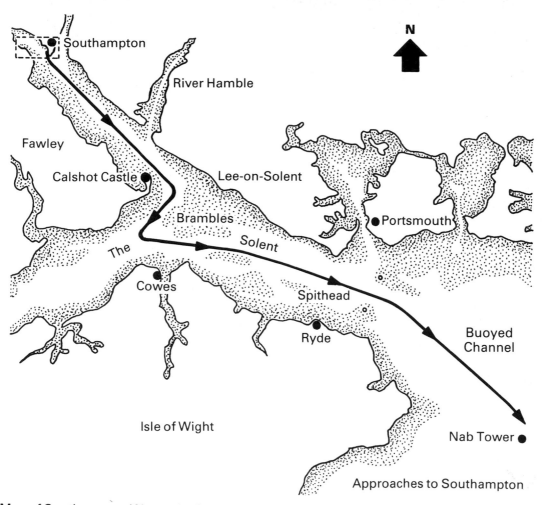

N

Southampton

River Hamble

Fawley

Calshot Castle

Lee-on-Solent

Brambles

Solent

The

Cowes

Spithead

Ryde

Portsmouth

Buoyed
Channel

Isle of Wight

Nab Tower

Approaches to Southampton

Map of Southampton Water, the Solent, Spithead and the Nab Tower, showing the ship's track to the English Channel

stream. Today the tide is ebbing (the ship can sail on any state of the tide) and again he will use a combination of Astern Pitch on the propellers, Bow Thrust and tugs to counteract this as needed. His successive commands will obviously vary according to changing conditions but a typical sequence might be:

'Zero Pitch Starboard.'

'Pitch One Port Astern.'

'Bow Thrust at half to port' (pushing the ship to starboard).

'After tugs pull Full Ahead.'

'Forward tugs pull Half Ahead.'

By steady process he gets the ship nicely positioned in the channel as the gap between ship and shore widens to a flurry of waving handkerchiefs from well-wishers ashore and a background of suitable 'sailing' music from the deck speakers.

Once satisfied with his position in the channel, the Pilot calls:

'After tugs come in and let go,' and promptly this is related to the Second Officer at the stern whose men prepare to release the lines, which are the property of the tug rather than the ship. As soon as the tugs have backed up sufficiently to slacken the lines, the stern party quickly takes the loops, or 'eyes', off the bitts (or posts) to let them fall to the water, whereupon both tugs move full ahead and winch in their lines to avoid any fouling of the ship's propellers.

Now the Pilot passes the order (relayed by the First Officer on Watch to his colleague forward) for one of the bow tugs to come in and let go, emphasising his need to be told when the boat is positioned for this. In the tug's interests caution is vital since the pronounced flair to the *QE2's* bow plates greatly restricts the Pilot's vision from the Bridge, and he is likely to see at best the tug's mast and funnel as she lies under the bow.

History relates numerous tragedies through precipitate action by the Bridge, when tugs have been toppled over to sink like stones with frequent loss of life. When the First Officer forward has reported the tug positioned for letting go, the Pilot, on his own frequency, orders: 'Let go *Calshot.*' The First Officer relays this to the forward mooring deck party who immediately remove the wire 'eye' from the bitt, letting the line fall to the water. The red-funnelled *Calshot* now steams full ahead to get clear and take in her line, leaving the sole remaining tug, the buff white and black-stacked *Albert* still holding the ship on a taut line forward.

The propellers are now at Pitch 2 Ahead, sufficient to maintain steerage way and keep the ship's head aligned on the channel. Swiftly the careful procedure is repeated for letting go the *Albert* and when she is reported 'All Clear' and visibly steaming away, the *QE2* slowly gathers way down channel. With all tugs clear, the Wing Party moves into the Wheelhouse, all controls being switched from former to latter. Now the Pilot calls to the Coxswain on the wheel:
'Steer one three zero.'
'One three zero,' repeats the Coxswain.
'Steady on one three zero, sir,' he adds as soon as he has the ship on the prescribed heading.

It is a meticulous ruling on all ships that the man on the wheel repeats each and every helm order to confirm that he has heard it correctly, speaking loudly and clearly, as well as verifying the course as soon as he has brought the ship to it. Now the Master says to the First Officer:
'Please tell Aft to let me know when they come abreast of the end of the quay,' then turning to the Pilot, in deference to the man who has the con:
'I'd like to blow three long blasts please.'
Aside from being a nice, time-honoured touch, the farewell blowing of the ship's siren is all good publicity. The Pilot promptly gives his assent and with the appropriate advice from the stern, the Master himself presses the button to sound the Tyfon air whistle located on the mast above. The three blasts of between four and six seconds each boom out – deeply resonant – across the water and the city of Southampton, whose citizens must by now be so accustomed to the sound of 'their' ship.

The tug *Albert* now replies with three similar blasts, a somewhat puny sound by comparison with the *basso profundo* of the big ship. At this point, many Masters may give a further, short blast, to which the tug will reply in kind, but our Captain believes this to be incorrect and bordering on the frivolous! Other Masters today have dropped the custom altogether, which is a pity – especially for the passengers and their well-wishers ashore who may regard it as the culminating moment of excitement – not to say emotion – of a departing liner.

Now the Master gives the command 'Anchor Party only forward', meaning that the forward mooring party as such stands down, leaving the carpenters standing by the capstans in the event that the anchors may be needed in a sudden emergency during the passage out to the Nab Tower. Similarly the Master now says 'Off stations aft' which the Staff Captain repeats to the Second Officer down aft, releasing that party for other duties.

The Chief Officer now appears on the Bridge to personally report to the Master that 'All shell doors are secure'.

To port, the elongated Netley Hospital slips by and with the ship now making some 9kt down the channel, the Esso Refinery at Fawley – hacked out of the New Forest – looms brightly ahead to starboard. It can be seen that there are three tankers berthed at the jetties: a large crude carrier and two much smaller product tankers loading refined oil products (hence their name) from the cluster of storage tanks on the shore. To the east of the channel, at anchor, lie other tankers awaiting their turn on the berths, and there is not a lot of room for *QE2* to pass. As a precaution the Pilot calls for 'Dead Slow Ahead' (Pitch 1 on the Combinator levers), which with a shaft speed of 72rpm reduces speed to about 5kt, at which the ship just maintains steerage way in the existing wind and tide conditions. Too much speed would have the effect of drawing the moored tankers away from the jetties, perhaps enough to even part their moorings, such as happened at the start of the first and only voyage of the ill-fated *Titanic* in 1912, as though a portent of what was to happen only days later.

As the Fawley Refinery passes astern, speed is increased to Slow Ahead (Pitch 2 on the Combinators), this returning to the previous speed of some 9kt. To port, in the darkness, lies the mouth of the Hamble River out of which small sailing craft may appear at any time of the day or night. All on the Bridge keep a wary eye lifted for any that may suddenly appear, their small navigation lights difficult to see with the myriad of background light from ashore. Fine on the port bow the large black mass of a Japanese car carrier looms ever closer and pilots of both vessels communicate with each other continuously on VHF radio until *QE2* is past and clear.

Calshot Castle and Spit now approaches on the starboard side, the area once renowned as a base for seaplanes and flying-boats. Beyond this Spit, stretching down to the Brambles Buoy, lies the notorious Thorn Channel, a veritable maritime 's' bend and *QE2* is, on this particular voyage, taking the easterly channel to the Nab Tower rather than the shorter westerly route out past the Needles rocks. The Thorn Channel is a particularly hazardous area to navigate for any large vessel and the Pilot uses all his expertise to counter wind and tide as he cons the ship through the turns, keeping the centreline of the ship as close as possible to the centreline of the channel.

Soon, the Brambles Buoy, marking the western extremity of the Brambles Bank, approaches on the port bow. There are some older members of *QE2's* shipboard staff who remember a fateful night in the 1950s when the great *Queen Elizabeth* was moving up from the Spithead for a night arrival at Southampton and was approaching Brambles Buoy when fog suddenly descended. In such conditions it was all too easy to misjudge the timing of the commencement of the turn and *Queen Elizabeth* grounded heavily on the Brambles Bank, steadfastly refusing all attempts to move her for several days until a massive fleet of tugs had assembled to float her clear on a spring tide with only minimal indentation to her bottom plating.

Today, however, all is very different, with a clear night sky and light westerly breeze. With the experience of many years behind him, and a well practised eye, the Pilot knows exactly at what point to commence the turn to port. The propulsion motors are still in Combinator Mode, which at 72rpm on Pitch 2 gives a speed of some 9 to 10kt.

'Hard a port,' calls the Pilot and the Helmsman dutifully obeys.

As the ship starts to swing the Pilot orders: 'Reduce to twenty,' and the helm is brought quickly from its hard a port position to 20° of port rudder.

As the vessel approaches her next new heading the order is given 'Midships!' and then 'Steady on one two zero,' each order being repeated by the Helmsman, and these are the only voices heard within the Wheelhouse at this time. When the ship is steady on the new course the Helmsman tells the Pilot, in a loud voice:

'Steady on one two zero, sir!'

Cowes, home of the famous Royal Yacht Squadron lies abeam on the starboard side. The Master now consults with the Pilot to see if the ship's speed could be safely increased so as to reduce the pilotage time and ensure all extra personnel employed in this late sailing departure can get to sleep as soon as possible, as arrival at Cherbourg is scheduled for 06.00hrs the next morning.

The Pilot agrees to the speed increase and after consulting with the First Engineer in the ECR,

both Combinator levers are moved from Pitch 4 to Pitch 6 in one clean and smooth movement. This movement of the Combinator levers enables the ship to achieve speeds of up to 20kt whilst ensuring the propulsion motors remain in the Synchro-Converter supply mode (this will be explained in greater detail later).

Ryde Pier now approaches to starboard and the low dark shoreline of Lee-on-the-Solent passes to port and the silhouette of the solid, cylindrical, structure of the Fort Blockhouse can be seen close on the port bow.

Within minutes the Pilot cons the ship through a gentle turn to starboard, steadying her on a course of 180° which will leave the Nab Tower at a distance of half-a-mile to port. He has reached the limit of his pilotage, and says as much informally but clearly to the Master. On this particular voyage the Pilot is not in fact disembarking but is travelling to Cherbourg, in an unofficial capacity, later to return to Southampton by ferry.

It is midnight and the Master, eager to get to his bed, gladly hands over the con to the Duty First Officer:

'You have the ship, Mr Moxom.'

At this time during any departure there are a thousand and one jobs to be done, the first being the securing of the anchors for the voyage, and this order is passed over the VHF walkie-talkie to the foc'sle party:

'For'd, Bridge!'

'For'd,' the Duty Carpenter replies.

'Island secure please.' This is a term peculiar to Cunard vessels reflecting the ship's frequent navigation of waters such as the Caribbean where short voyages between islands in sheltered waters is the norm. Heavy steel bars are dropped across the anchor cables, and the massive capstan-like cable lifters are left in gear with the brakes hove up tight. The more permanent wire lashings are not used in this procedure. When the anchors are secure the Carpenter reports back to the Bridge:

'All secure for'd,' whereupon the Officer of the Watch advises them to stand down and reminds them that standby time in the morning is 06.00hrs.

The Second Officer has been busily employed plotting the ship's position, on the chart, throughout the pilotage and he now plots the departure position for 00.00hrs, the time given to the ECR as Official Departure Time. From this position all distances, times and hence fuel calculations will be made.

The First Officer is in the forefront of the Wheelhouse watching radar, compass and engine speed settings whilst still maintaining a visual lookout. The Duty Coxswain provides an extra

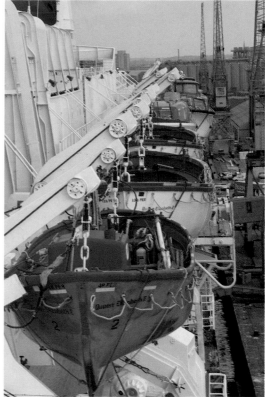

Above left:
**QE2 lies secure at her berth —
Southampton.**

Left:
**The Blue Ensign flies proudly
from the stern denoting that the
QE2's Master is a serving Captain
in the Royal Navy Reserve.**

Above left:
**As the sun sets over Southampton
the decklights illuminate the
vessel.**

Above right:
**The port Boat Deck, viewed from
the Bridge wing.**

Right:
**Tugs away: QE2 heads down
Southampton Water (viewed on a
previous voyage).**

pair of eyes for this — probably the most uninteresting but most important — part of the job. To date, there is not a radar system built that can 'see' wooden or fibreglass (commonly known as 'Tupperware') small craft, particularly when there is a sea running and craft such as these are invariably hidden in the troughs.

Watertight doors that had to be closed throughout the vessel's pilotage are now opened, with the exception of those few that must be closed and locked at sea because of their importance in protecting large open spaces such as cargo holds.

An ETA message is sent by telex to the Cherbourg agents advising them of our unchanged, scheduled arrival time of 07.00hrs local time at the Pilot station, and intended alongside time of 08.00hrs. This latter time is of vital importance as mooring gangs, stevedores etc must be ordered so that no overtime is paid if the ship is in fact berthed prior to 08.00hrs and the shore gangs then commence work before their allotted start time.

Many other routine tasks are also completed at this time and with the ship eerily quiet, save for the rustling of the breeze across the decks, the Bridge Officers settle into a long-established watchkeeping routine.

The direct-line distance to Cherbourg is 65nm from the Nab Tower, which for an 06.00hrs arrival would require a speed of only 9.2kt and so, at times like this, the ship will reduce speed and will, perhaps, run on just one shaft, thus saving fuel.

Although France, as most of Europe, maintains a time zone one hour ahead of that in the UK and, as QE2 is only calling in Cherbourg for a few hours, it is not prudent to advance the ship's clocks before arrival as it would then be necessary to retard clocks six hours over a five-night period during the voyage to New York.

The outer anchorages and approaches south of the Nab Tower are quiet this night and only the two Watch Officers and the Duty Coxswain remain on the Bridge. With the ship settling down to her reduced speed setting on the port shaft there is time for a cup of coffee and a few minutes respite before the next session of increased activity, that of crossing the westbound lane of the Channel Traffic Separation Scheme. The direct-line course of 204° takes QE2 across the westbound traffic lane, which all ships travelling down channel must follow, and some three-and-a-half miles to the west of EC2 (East Channel 2) Buoy before crossing the up-channel eastbound traffic lane and finally approaching Cherbourg.

Map of ship's track to Cherbourg from Southampton showing Channel Shipping lanes

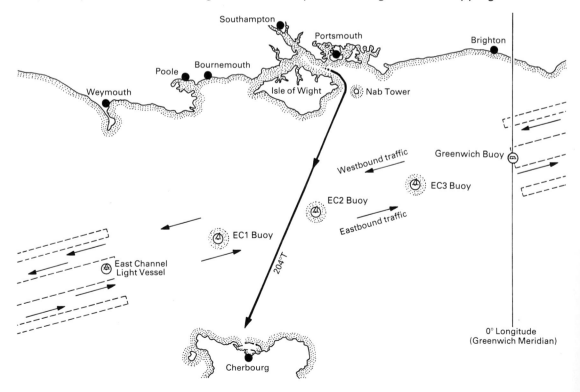

Cherbourg

It is now past 05.30hrs on a calm clear morning. The cross-channellers are beginning to sense a mood of anti-climax, realising that the few hours of high life are all but over as the coastline of the Cotentin peninsula looms ever closer — perhaps some wives persuading their husbands that next summer they must do the thing properly and book for the entire voyage.

Up on the Bridge as the ship approaches a position some five miles from the Fairway buoy, the First Officer contacts the ECR and requests Combinator Mode, having gradually reduced the setting on the levers to less than '4' — Pitch 4 being the maximum setting allowable at 72rpm in Combinator Mode. Earlier on, the ECR has brought the starboard shaft into service and with five engines on line since 05.00hrs speed was increased to about 20kt. The main propulsion motors are salient pole synchronous ac motors rated 44,000kW at 144rpm and are designed for variable frequency starting using synchro-converters rated 11,000kW at 144rpm. At the low speed of 72rpm (Combinator Mode) the output of the converters is restricted to 5,500kW. Thus it can be seen that when in Combinator Mode at Pitch 4, a maximum power setting of 5,500kW is available; but if pitch is increased in a single smooth movement to '6' then 11,000kW of power is available and revolutions increase to 144 enabling the ship to obtain a speed of at least 20kt, but still remain in Combinator Mode for instant manoeuvring. The QE2's engines will be discussed in more detail elsewhere.

The Master appears on the Bridge, and after listening to his First Officer's operational update turns to the Second Officer of the Watch who has been busily employed in plotting the vessel's position on the British Admiralty Chart. 'Very good', says the Master and turning to the First Officer says:
'I have the con Mr Hyde-Liniker. Call up the Pilots please and inform them that we will have the ladder on the starboard side.'

The message is passed over by VHF radio to the Pilot launch on a prescribed frequency. The Second Officer now leaves the Bridge to supervise the opening of the shell door on No 5 Deck through which the Pilot will embark by way of a short rope ladder with broad wooden rungs.

As the ship slips past the Fairway buoy, the First Officer establishes the precise arrival time and the duration of the run from the Nab Tower with the ECR. The Pilot launch closes rapidly, beginning her wide turn to approach the Pilot ladder. The Second Coxswain leaves the Wheelhouse and goes up on the Flag Deck to commence raising the flags for the vessel's arrival. First to be hoisted is the French tricolour, a courtesy shown to the country whose waters and eventually whose port a vessel is entering, followed by the Cunard houseflag, Queen's Award flag, International codeletter 'H' signalling that the vessel has a Pilot onboard, and finally the Blue Ensign which will be exchanged for a similar Blue Ensign flown from aft when the first mooring line is fast ashore.

The powerful Pilot launch now edges her way alongside the shell door and placing her fendered bow against the hull plating matches her speed to that of the ship so as to enable the Pilot easy access to the ladder. High up on the Boat Deck passengers watch as the Pilot clambers aboard, the launch chuntering away at full speed as soon as all is clear. The Second Officer greets the Pilot with a cheery 'Bonjour Capitaine' and immediately turns toward the steel door that leads to No 5 Deck and the Bridge beyond.

During the Second Officer's sojourn from the Bridge all watertight doors will again have been closed for arrival and so the Pilot must be guided along No 4 Deck to the forward elevators. Upon his arrival in the Wheelhouse he greets the Master, who informs him of the ship's course, present speed and any other information he deems relevant before handing over the con. The Pilot nods his consent and immediately asks for

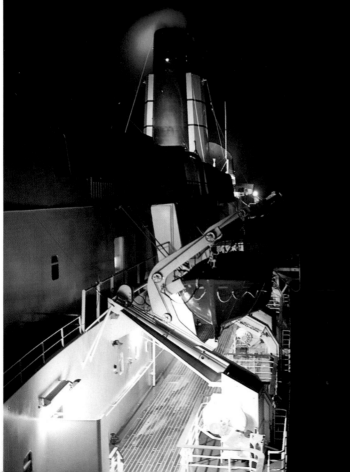

Above:
Captain Alan Bennell and Pilot, Mr Dan Robson, con the vessel through the narrow confines of Southampton water.

Left:
The port Boat Deck at night.

Inset right:
Passengers relax at dinner in the Mauretania Restaurant. *Cunard*

Right:
The Isle of Wight closes to starboard as *QE2* heads east towards Nab Tower in the last rays of the day's sun. *Cunard*

Above left:
Passenger launch *Alpha*: viewed from the helicopter deck.

Above right:
Dusk approaches over the North Atlantic: a rare calm evening.

Left:
The Grande Lounge. *Cunard*

Right:
The port Bridge wing consul.

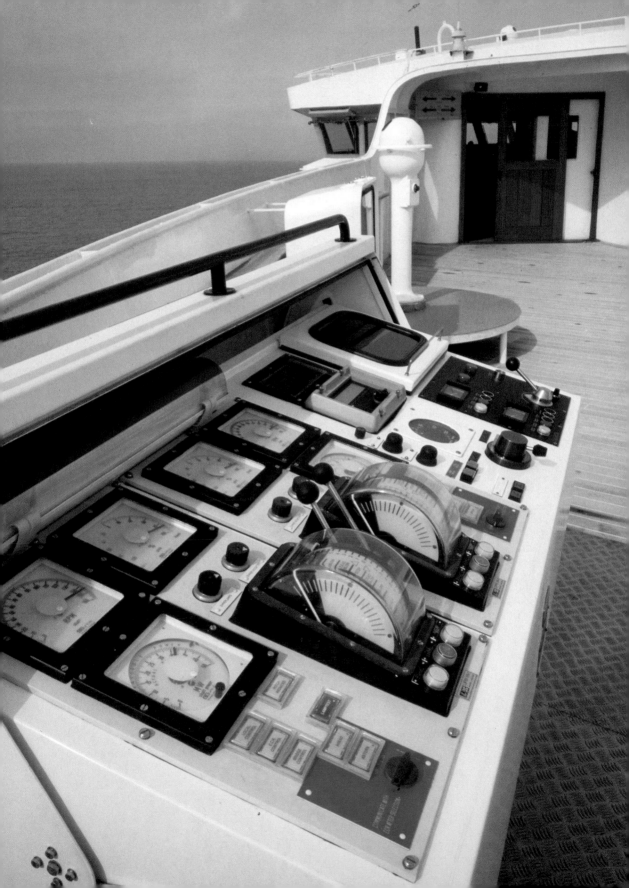

The Voyage — Day 1

On the dawn of the next day, with Bishop Rock lying well to the east, *Queen Elizabeth 2* is making a steady 29kt through moderate seas. Thanks to the fine lines and the 'bulb' beneath the waterline at her forefoot, the bow wave and wash seem minimal for a ship of this size and power — a far cry from her illustrious predecessor the hefty *Queen Mary* whose huge creaming bow wave heralded her approach no sooner had she hove up on the horizon.

It is 08.00hrs and the attractively headed daily programme *The Leisure World of QE2* has been slipped under the door of each of the 951 passenger cabins along with a daily news sheet printed onboard, courtesy of 20th century satellite technology. The continuous programme of events for the entertainment of passengers has already begun with the daily quiz available in sheet form from the ship's library. A prize is awarded for the first correct, or nearest correct solution, handed in to the librarian before 15.00hrs.

By this time most passengers are well into their breakfast in either of the restaurants, although some elect to eat in the privacy of their cabins.

Up on the Bridge the First and Second Officers of the 8-12 Watch are hard at work, surrounded by a wealth of navigational aids. The term 'aids' is appropriate as all the equipment 'aids' the Navigator in determining various aspects of the ship's status. From actual position on the earth's surface to the amount of set and drift being experienced, to the course and distance to next waypoint etc. Regrettably, the term 'aids' in modern times tends to be understood as something far from navigational terminology, but seamen in general are well known for their sense of humour on any subject matter.

Essentially the Bridge is the province of the Deck Dept as opposed to the Technical, although it can be seen by some — ignorant to the ways of the sea — as a mere lookout post! Historically there has existed between the Deck and Engine Depts — both in the Royal and Merchant Navies — a distinct vacuum: oil and water never mix, or so the old adage goes, but in the 1980s things have changed. The age did exist, when a Chief engineer lined up his men, on the first day of a voyage, and pointing to an imaginary line on the deck stated that his side of the line was the only side that existed for engineers and crossing into the 'Deckies' space would never be tolerated. This was particularly so from the social aspect as

Below:
Broadcasts to the passengers around the ship are made at various times, in particular immediately prior to departure, at 09.30hrs and noon each day, during Emergency Drills and at any other time when interesting or relevant information is to be passed on.

Here, Second Officer Ian McNaught makes such an announcement, which often results in telephone calls to the Bridge from confused passengers, requesting a 'Geordie-to-English' translation book . . .

engineers traditionally had their own accommodation and bar/lounge area, well away from those of the Deck Dept.

Happily those days are passed, although some diehards would not agree that it was for the better. Today's engineer and navigator have to work in close harmony with each other as many aspects of their jobs overlap even more so than they did 15 years ago. The Master Mariner of today has to pass a 3hr written paper on engineering and control systems which does in fact represent one-fifth of the total written examinations for a Master's Certificate. Without a good working knowledge of the machinery and propulsion system in general, today's Navigating Officer would be at a loss when attempting to operate a Bridge Control system such as that aboard *QE2*.

QE2 proudly boasts what is, probably, the largest complement of Master Mariners on any vessel afloat. Out of the 16 officers employed (from the Captain and relief Captain down through to the junior of the Second Officers), 13 are Master Mariners and two are presently sitting their examinations. Promotion is traditionally slow, and many Captains joke that they never walk down stairs ahead of any Junior Officer lest the 'hand of fate' is tempted to propel them downwards and thus the Junior Officer upwards.

Bridge Instrumentation

The endless array of Navigational Aids (Navaids) and instruments on the Bridge almost beggar description. Along and set against the forward bulkhead of the Wheelhouse, beneath the long rank of inward-sloping windows, each with its massive wiper, stretches a cream-coloured con-

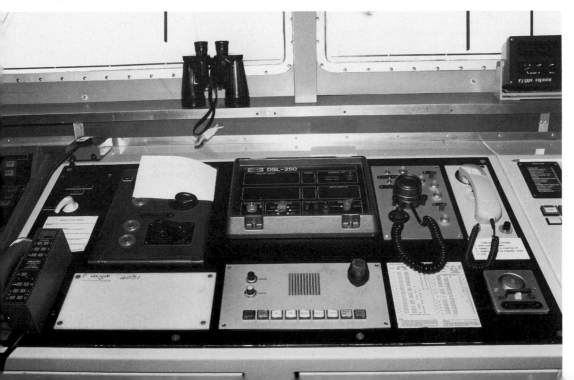

Below:
The port end of the Bridge Console showing, from left to right, VHF Radio Telephone, Tyfon whistle controls, the Doppler Log with talk-back to the ECR (Engine Control Room) and SCR (Safety Control Room) below it. At top right are the talk-backs to the forward and aft mooring decks and a sound-powered telephone to the Steering Gear Compartment.

Above:
QE2 proceeds slowly towards Cherbourg Pilot Station. *Cunard*

Left:
The foc'sle head — showing storeroom 'mushroom' ventilation trunks in the foreground and anchor cable lifters in the background.

Right:
From the foc'sle head looking aft with the ship's spare 'bower' anchor in foreground.

sole newly fitted in Bremerhaven. On this lies much of the equipment needed to drive this, the most famous of all the great liners. From port to starboard along this console are:

● One of the three VHF Radio Telephones required for ship-to-shore or ship-to-ship communications and also to maintain a listening watch on the International Distress VHF Channel 16.

● The Tyfon whistle controls for the three whistle systems. Two whistles are located on the mainmast directly above the Bridge (one electric and the other air operated). The third is situated high above the foredeck right in the forepart of the vessel, and this electrically operated whistle is the one used in restricted visibility to sound one prolonged blast at intervals not exceeding 2min and is activated by an automatic timer. Those who recall travelling in the single cabins immediately beneath the fore funnel of the old *Queen Mary* should appreciate this! Not only was the blast of the twin sirens devastating, but also the furniture shook so much that sleep was out of the question.

● To the right of the whistle controls lies the Raytheon DSL-250 Dopler Speed Log. This machine gives a very accurate readout of speed over the ground, and through the water, depending on water depth. Narrow beams of energy are transmitted from the bottom of the ship at 30° from the vertical line. Echoes from these transmissions are received and

processed to produce a true speed of the ship. In water sufficiently shallow to permit reliable receipt of echoes from the seabed, the log will indicate ship's speed over the ground and also the depth of water under the hull in either feet, metres or fathoms (6ft = 1 fathom). In deep water the system will detect reflections from the water mass and will therefore show speed through the water which must then have any current or tide applied to it to obtain a true speed made good over the ground.

● Below and extending to the right of the Dopler Log are the talk-back systems to the Engine Control Room (ECR), Safety Control Room (SCR), Bridge Wings and mooring decks forward and aft. Also, a powerless telephone is incorporated into the system in case of power failure.

● Next come the Main Engine Generator status board and alarm systems. Many of these alarms and emergency stops have been deemed to be unnecessary to the Bridge operation and since have been disconnected. To maintain the aesthetic character of the console, the redundant buttons were kept *in situ*. A certain navigator took it upon himself to redesignate these buttons as 'onboard defence systems', which often brings a smile to the face of many a visiting passenger and

Below:
The central portion of the Bridge console showing Combinator Levers and Pitch, Power and Revolution Indicators.

occasionally a look of sheer alarm as the accompanying officer's finger strays toward the button marked 'Captain's Ejector Seat'!

The emergency crash stops for the propulsion motors are also located here as is the steering gear motor indicators and electric tiller lever.

- The remainder, and in fact the majority of the console, is given over to propulsion. Gauges showing shaft speeds, percentage pitch on each propeller, electrical power used and available, and are placed above the main Combinator levers which control the pitch and therefore the power being supplied to each propeller. The 'Mode' selectors are located either side of the Combinator levers.

- At the far starboard end lies the Bow Thruster control panel. There are two Bow Thruster units which lie in two tunnels right in the forepart of the vessel about 20ft below the waterline. Within each tunnel lies a propeller capable of varying its pitch from 50% to 100%, depending on how much traverse thrust is required. Each propeller is driven by a 1,000hp electric motor through an elbow drive. When not in use, thick steel doors at the outer ends of the tunnels are closed electronically — flush with the outer hull. The thrusters are used only at speeds of below 8kt. Their effectiveness is:

Knots
0-2 — 100%
2-4 — 75%
4-6 — 50%
6-8 — 25%
Above 8 — zero

- Slightly aft of the forward console and on the centreline of the ship sits the all-important Sperry Autopilot. At this moment — in open sea and clear conditions — the Autopilot is engaged, the Coxswain on Watch remains constantly alert for the switching to hand steering should circumstances demand it. The sudden appearance of a myriad of small wooden fishing boats many miles from land is a fairly regular occurrence, and a combination of non-detection by radar — because of their construction and size — and a moderate or rough sea, resulting in a later visible detection by lookouts, has caused many a mariner to return to hand steering and con his vessel safely through the fleet, often reducing speed to do so if time permits.

Gone are the days of solid oak wheels with brass trim. The coxswain today will use a wheel not greatly larger than that of a cabin cruiser or may instead use the small electric

Below:
The starboard end of the console houses the Bow Thruster control and yet another telephone!

Bottom:
'This clock is running a bit slow!'
'Yes Ian. That's because it is the Autopilot!'

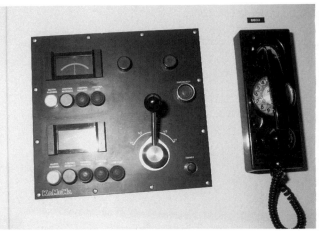

49

Far left:
The bright sun belies the chill of the Lido Deck on an early transatlantic morning.

Below left:
West Atlantic sunset: viewed from the port Bridge wing.

Left:
Once around the Boat Deck is 1/5th of a mile: keep on jogging.

Below:
QE2 at full speed in calm waters. *Cunard*

tiller lever no more than 2in in length.

- The Autopilot is in turn linked to one of the two Sperry Gyro Compasses each of which consists mainly of a free gyroscope, controlled to the extent that its spin axis constantly seeks to align itself with the local meridian. The interior rotor turns at a speed of 1,200rpm and remains free from the influence of any external force, thus providing an entirely true heading for the ship.

Gyro Compasses nowadays are no larger than a small car battery but in years past resembled something out of *Star Wars* and as such were held in great dread by the ship's Navigator. The interior rotor could well have exceeded 18in in diameter and weighed over 100lb. The Gyro Compass would live in its own small room close to the Bridge and to approach it for maintenance — or for whatever reason — knowing there was enough energy in that spinning rotor to send it and you into orbit, was enough to make a grown man weak at the knees.

It was not unusual for older Gyro Compasses to reverse themselves through 180°, and one ship, in the early 1960s, discovered this to its chagrin. Two days out of New York, on an eastbound voyage home, during the early hours the Gyro Compass reversed itself and the ship completed a 180° turn under Autopilot without anyone noticing. It was overcast and raining heavily with a moderate sea and swell. Some 24hr later the sun rose in the west and questions started to be asked! Least of all by a bewildered charterer in England who just could not understand how the Captain could be two days late on a seven-day voyage with relatively fine weather forecast. To make matters even worse the Chief Engineer, a usually dour individual, had persuaded the Radio Officer to send a personal telegram to the company's Operations Manager advising him that 'No breakdowns of any kind had occurred this voyage'! Of course when the truth emerged, dismissals were inevitable and both the Captain and the Navigator (ironically it was on his watch the incident occurred) lost their jobs. Nowadays, Gyro Compasses are maintenance-free sealed units with a virtual 100% reliability.

- Immediately behind the steering position there is a walk-around screen stretching from

Below:
The Magnavox Satellite Omega Navigator.

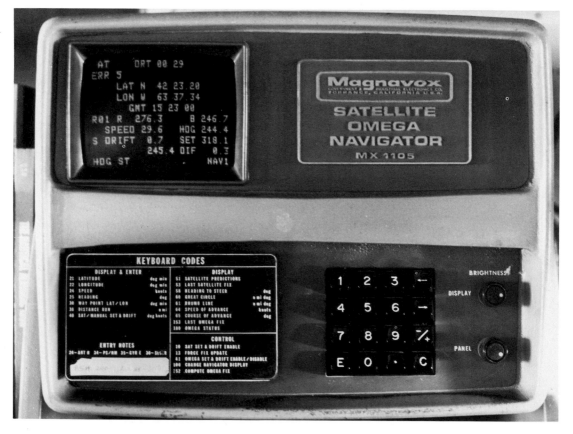

deck to deckhead, giving protection from the anglepoise lamps set over a long chart-table. Above this table sits the three main Navigational Aids — namely the Satellite Receiver, the Decca Navigator and the Loran Receiver.

● The MX 1105 Magnavox Satellite Navigator receives signals from satellites in orbit around the earth. There are at present six operational satellites on segmented polar orbits. Each satellite transmits a 399.968MHz signal. The onboard receiver reproduces an exact 400MHz signal. When compared to the incoming satellite transmission the resulting 32kHz signal, which is affected by Doppler Effect, is used to determine the vessel's position with an accuracy of plus or minus 300ft. The accurate timing of the system as a whole is undertaken by atomic clocks in series, thus ensuring exceptionally accurate timings.

An elderly American passenger, during a rare Bridge visit, listened to the explanation of the system by the Second Officer, and proudly stated to all and sundry that 'Their goddam clock is a second out' and wouldn't it be a good idea to change the batteries as they appeared to be running slow! The Officer politely agreed and the passenger departed the Bridge, pleased that he had found something at fault that none of these bright young men had noticed!

● The Loran C (an abbreviation for Long Range Navigational System Mk C) receiver, is a familiar Navaid in modern vessels, and is used for position fixing. The system uses pulsed transmissions on a particular frequency and consists of a Master station and up to four 'Slaves' that transmit synchronised signals. On the Bridge, the Loran C tracks and measures the time delay between each Slave station, arriving at an accurate position by such means. The distance, on the earth's surface between Master station and each Slave station is in the order of 600nm and given favourable atmospheric conditions, it is possible to obtain a reasonably accurate fix 1,500/2,000 miles from any station.

● The celebrated Decca Navigator operates on nearly the same frequency as the Loran C. Primarily for inshore waters navigation, the Decca Receiver provides a highly accurate aid in such surroundings, operating on a continual wave phase comparison basis — again between a Master station and three Slave stations. Like the Loran, it also lays a grid of radio signals over the earth's surface, and these are reproduced on the British Admiralty Charts for each area of coverage.

● Above the Wheelhouse, on the 'Monkey Island' standing in a small recessed deck of its own is the Magnetic Compass Binnacle. Every ship must carry a Magnetic Compass by law as it is the rarity among today's proliferation of electronic gadgetry in that it does not rely on an external power source to operate it. It just sits there, year after year, pointing — as far as 'it' is aware — to Magnetic North. Budding Master Mariners know of its capabilities and eccentricities only too well, as a large proportion of their Oral Examination and an even larger proportion of the 3hr Navigational Instruments written examination is on Magnetic Compass work.

● Comforting, to sufferers of seasickness, is the sight of the controls for the stabilisers. Manufactured by Denny-Brown, *QE2* has two pairs of stabilising fins — one pair just forward of midships and the other pair aft of that. They are retracted into recesses in the

Below:
Not something out of *Star Wars* – although many college students think it might be – but the Lilley & Gillie Magnetic Compass Binnacle.

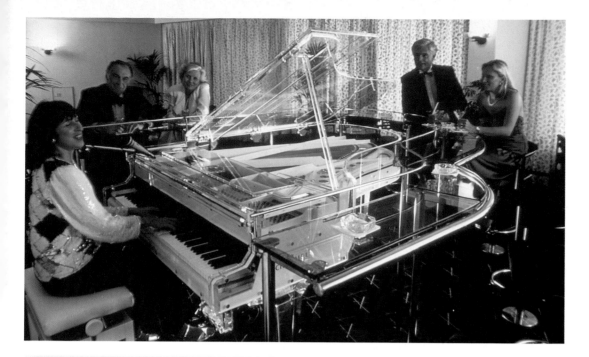

Left:
The Helicopter Deck provides a sun trap for the hardy.

Above:
Arline Daniels entertains at the piano in the Yacht Club Bar. *Cunard*

Below:
The Boat Deck illuminations seen against the back drop of the Verazzano Narrows Bridge-New York.

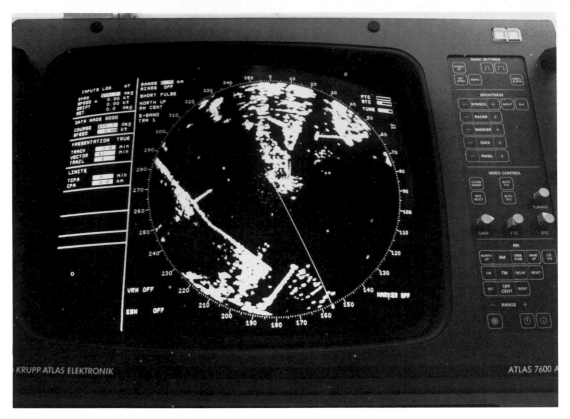

hull when not in use and are extended for most of the time when at sea. They fold out from the recesses and are locked in position at 90° to the hull and resemble miniature aircraft wings. Their cross-sectional profile is very much wing-shaped and, as the gyroscopic control system senses the amount of rolling force being applied to the ship, it sends a signal to the fins to alter their angle of attack to the sea by pivoting either up or down to create an upthrust on the downroll side and a downthrust on the uproll side, thus damping the roll by as much as 60%.

The stabilisers only extend about 15ft from the hull but are extremely efficient in their roll-damping capabilities. When 'working' hard in rough seas, they do cause a small amount of drag which can reduce the ship's speed by up to ½kt. They are folded-in before arrival at port, as it would be very embarrassing to find that the ship lies 15ft off the quayside when berthed. Asking 1,800 passengers to jump the gap does not augur well for good public relations.

It is quite common for the stabiliser controls and Bow Thrust controls to be linked in such a way that it is not possible to give power to the Bow Thrusters whilst the 'fins'

Above:
The Krupp Atlas 7600 ARPA radar showing the view down Southampton Water from *QE2's* berth.

are still out. The Bow Thrusters can only be used at slow speeds — when berthing or manoeuvring in inshore waters — and at times such as these the stabilisers would not be required.

● The Radar system aboard *Queen Elizabeth 2* is 'state-of-the-art' and comprises of two Krupp Atlas (German) ARPA radars with interswitch capabilities. ARPA stands for Automatic Radar Plotting Aid and it is a requirement by law to carry such equipment. The two display units are the 8600 and the 7600 daylight viewing radars and are second to none in their display clarity, efficiency of operation and design capabilities. Either unit can operate on ranges from as small as 0.25 miles up to 72 miles on either 3 or 10cm wavebands. The map storage facility, within the computer memory, enables chartlets of ports and their approaches to be retained for recall whenever required and frequently — in conditions of restricted visibility — enable the ship to enter ports that might otherwise mean she would have to anchor off to await clearer weather.

Above:
QE2's new funnel, fatter by design to hold the nine exhaust gas boilers in each engine uptake. Note the 'scoops' on either side at the base which cause a substantial updraught, when underway, which causes the flue gases to be expelled up and away from the ship.

Only a small fraction of the units' capabilities are at present being utilised, but finances have been requested to expand the system to include GPS (Global Positioning Satellite) Navigation input to enable immediate referencing of maps to an accuracy of ±25m. This could in turn be linked to an illuminated chart-table display that could take any size of Mercator Chart and would constantly indicate ship's position by means of a laser light-spot from beneath the chart.

Stretching to port and starboard of the Wheelhouse, on the open deck, are the Bridge Wings, commanding unobstructed views forward and aft. At the outer extremity of each wing is a raised deck for better vision overside when berthing. On each raised deck is a control console containing duplicate engine, rudder and Bow Thruster controls.

Above:
The mainmast, showing from bottom to top: the DF aerial loops, the 3cm radar scanner, the 10cm scanner, and the electric and air-controlled whistle horns.

Above:
Executive Chef Rudi Sodamin and his team show just some of the delights on offer at the daily lunch time buffet. *Cunard*

Left:
Manhattan at dawn.

Above right:
The Statue of Liberty with the twin towers of the World Trade Centre in the background.
Cunard

Right:
Approaching the berth at Pier 90.

In 1953, a celebrated Cunard Master — somewhat short in stature — berthed the huge *Queen Mary* at New York without the aid of tugs. He achieved this daunting task with the help of a wooden crate on which to stand, making history and creating a jam of monumental proportions along the Westside Highway — to the fury of the Manhattan Police Dept.

Bridge Officers

The three First Officers, each holding a Foreign Going Master's Certificate are, along with the three Second Officers, the Watchkeepers on the Bridge. The traditional Watch system of 4hr on, 8hr off is maintained every day of the year,

Below:
The ship's whistles are tested every day at noon and the first blast indicates the time of noon exactly. Deck Boy Kieran Marchant braves the North Atlantic elements to test the Bridge wing whistle controls.

Below right:
QE2 carries 20 lifeboats with a total capacity of 2,244 persons.

whether in port or at sea, and with a First and Second Officer on each Watch *Queen Elizabeth 2* is the only vessel left afloat that can proudly boast such a wealth of Master Mariners.

The most senior of the First Officers is effectively the Chief Officer's deputy and does in fact frequently sail as Relief Chief Officer. His prime duty is that of Senior Watchkeeper on the 4-8 Watch, both mornings and evenings, and is also responsible for all Continuous Survey work required for DoT inspections regarding tanks and structure and fire doors and dampers, the latter being contained within eight fire zones and surveyed at frequent intervals.

The Intermediate First Officer keeps the 8-12 Watch, once again both mornings and evenings and along with the Second Officer on his Watch is responsible for all aspects of lifesaving appliances including the maintenance and upkeep of 20 lifeboats, 56 liferafts and two large passenger launches.

The Junior First Officer is the ship's Navigator and is directly responsible to the Master for all aspects of the vessel's navigation. From courses and distances for each voyage to future schedul-

ing and itineraries. His job, although most important, is in fact the least involved and is therefore delegated to the most junior of the First Officers.

The Senior Second Officer keeps the 4-8 Watch and is the Senior First's assistant when survey work is to be carried out. He is also responsible, directly, to the Chief Officer for stability calculations which are now completed with the aid of an IBM computer.

The Junior Second Officer is invariably the newest recruit and to him is therefore delegated jobs such as Public Relations Officer, Met Officer and Cargo Officer. It is also his responsibility to make the entries in the Official Logbook, a Government document recording important

Right:
Capt Alan Bennell and Second Officer Ian McNaught discuss a future call at Barcelona.

Below:
Passenger launch *Alpha* which, along with launch *Beta*, can carry up to 240 passengers at a time. These launches are used solely at 'Launch Ports' where, because of her size, *QE2* has to anchor offshore.

Far left:
QE2 lies secure alongside Pier 90, New York.

Below:
Approaching Fawley Oil Refinery — outward bound — Southampton (previous voyage).

events aboard ship from inspections of crew accommodation by the Master to testing of the steering gears prior to departure from port.

All First Officers, and also Second Officers who hold a Master's Certificate, wear two-and-a-half gold stripes on their tunic sleeves. Second Officers holding just a Mate's Certificate wear two stripes.

Heading West

The English Channel is now far behind, and the ship is currently on course to make the Ambrose Light outside New York Harbour by 04.00hrs on the following Wednesday, involving the minimum possible steaming distance.

While historically Masters had their individual ideas of how to achieve this, the *Titanic* disaster of 1912 resulted in certain agreement (rather than regulation) on the navigation of specific tracks to and from North America in the interests of greater safety. These were adhered to generally until the end of World War 2 when advanced radar aids led to their relaxation (though sadly not preventing the fatal collision off Nantucket in 1956 of the ill-starred Italian liner *Andrea Doria* and the Swedish *Stockholm*).

Today the *QE2* broadly follows the Great Circle Route, taking her from Bishop's Rock to a position off southern Newfoundland, the gaunt

Virgin Rocks which lie to the south and slightly east of Cape Race. From there she will steer to the south of Sable Island, not much more than a large, scrubby sandbank lying off the southern shore of Nova Scotia.

At one time this uninviting place attained fame when a ship carrying a consignment of horses as part cargo, stranded there and a number of these intrepids struggled ashore to form an equine colony for some years, until finally succumbing to the elements.

From this position the ship takes a heading directly to the Nantucket Light lying off the historic island of that name near the Massachusetts coast. At one time this light was based on a manned vessel which also attained fame when in 1935, during fog, it was mortally struck by the White Star liner *Olympic* with tragic loss of life. Its replacement, another manned ship, lasted until 1962 when a new and more powerful light — automatically operated — was floated on a moored buoy, and remains there to date. From Nantucket, on the last leg of her sea voyage, the *QE2* heads for the Ambrose Light marking the seaward end of the channel into New York Harbour. Like Nantucket, the Ambrose Light was

at one time based on a manned vessel, until the 1960s when a tower was constructed on stilts to house the new light.

In this early stage of the voyage — less than 24hr out of Cherbourg — weather forecasts for the Western Atlantic will be keenly studied. If a storm is forecast lying across the ship's track, judgement is called for on the extent of the diversion that could be needed to avoid either damage or unnecessary discomfort to her passengers. Into such consideration would also come the implications of late arrival in New York and the attendant inconveniences. An immediate, additional workload would be laid on an already busy Purser's office, ascertaining from those many passengers travelling onwards from New York their ongoing travel arrangements, and the rearranging of such, involving copious messages to and from Cunard's Fifth Avenue offices. People are often not at their best when faced by delay, and patience may be needed on the part of the hard-pressed Purser's staff with some of the more irascible customers. Beyond this, consideration must be given to the passengers embarking in New York for the return trip, and the likely need to contact them for postponement of the existing embarkation time at the pier. Thus, as the ship progresses westward, the Master will continue to scrutinise the forecasts in a constant endeavour to track the likely course of

Above:
The Bridge – viewed from the foredeck showing the forward electric whistle on its tripod and both anchor cables leading into the hawsepipes where they connect onto each of the 12-tonne anchors.

Below:
A daily ritual is the noon speech, by the Captain and 12-4 Watch Second Officer. Here, Capt Alan Bennell and Second Officer Graham Starkey discuss the speech format.

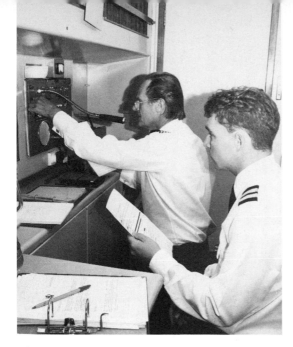

Above:
With preliminary discussions completed it's time to talk to the public!

Below:
Over 40 years old, the Mufax Weather Fax Receiver originated from the old *Queen Elizabeth.*

At lower right can be seen the new electronic Furuno Weather Fax Receiver. Together, these two machines provide a comprehensive supply of weather information.

the storm, hoping that it might just blow itself out before the ship reaches the area.

That perennial nuisance to transatlantic navigators — fog, in the region of the Grand Banks of Newfoundland — is always a strong possibility for encounter. This is the direct result of the meeting of the cold Labrador current with the warmer Gulf Stream, and the Master knows that at some point when in that vicinity he may well have to remain on the Bridge for long hours on end, as the powerful Tyfon on the foredeck blares out its warning every 2min. With memories of the *Titanic* showing little sign of dying, passengers may sense apprehension for the menace of drifting ice, although this has been greatly lessened by modern radar systems plus the extreme efficiency of the International Ice Patrol — formed shortly after the death of the White Star mammoth in 1912. The major burden of this service falls upon the Canadian and US Coastguard services, whose cutters, helicopters and advanced radar equipment maintain a constant search for bergs, growlers or thicker ice formation. Ice reports in any vicinity are transmitted from ship or aircraft to shore stations on the northeastern seaboard which promptly co-ordinate and repeat them for the benefit of ships approaching the ice area. If, at this early stage of the voyage, the *QE2* received a report of ice lying significantly to the south of the Virgin Rocks, the Master would keep a wary eye on its progress, assessing if eventual diversion would be necessary. One thing is a certainty:

Right:
**Capt Alan Bennell RD*RNR,
Master, *Queen Elizabeth 2.***

Below:
**The first iceberg sighted visually
– as opposed to an unidentified
radar target – from *QE2* in 20
years of transatlantic travel.**

under no circumstances would he contemplate navigating the ship through ice, for no hull form — barring those especially strengthened — is impervious to jagged shafts such as ripped open the *Titanic* over a length of five compartments — unsinkable as the ship was said to be.

Given the differing conditions with which he may be faced, the North Atlantic Master must also be a master in the art of crystal gazing.

At 10.15 on this first morning at sea, the alarm bells call the passengers to lifeboat drill, the Master having expressly requested the attendance of everybody at this highly vital practice for what to do in emergency. Following the instructions clearly posted in every cabin, passengers are expected to don lifejackets and warm clothing and muster at their prescribed boat stations (also indicated in all cabins). There they will have their jackets checked and adjusted if necessary and receive instruction from the officer in charge of their station on the precise

Left:
Having altered course slightly to afford the passengers a better view of the berg, *QE2* resumes her course towards Nantucket Light.

Below:
The Queen's Grill Lounge is situated on the Boat Deck.
Cunard

Above right:
Crew members arrive at their lifeboat stations during an Emergency Drill.

drill for the evacuation of the ship. Without lowering to the water, boats may be cleared away from their davits and swung outboard, ready to embark passengers at Promenade Deck level. Often at these boat drills, friendships are struck for the remainder of the voyage — sometimes the very reverse!

Onboard Entertainment

On stand-down from lifeboat drill, the day's programme of events is resumed with gusto. An impressive variety of entertainment to suit most tastes follows throughout this and each successive day of the crossing, and at this point it would be appropriate to describe the full range and scope of such activity.

Given the level of competition in the cruise industry generally and the high status of Cunard within it, careful selection for quality is important. The Entertainments Manager in New York has years of experience in this field, assisted by selected agents in the locating of a variety of acts for performance aboard the ship, where the

Cruise Director has the overall responsibility for their programming and switching between the public rooms from day to day. Needless to say that he will be vociferous in complaint if any act fails to meet standards, so that screening and selection by the agent are of ultra importance.

Taking music first, there are two top-class dance bands playing nightly in each of the two principal showrooms, the Grand Lounge and the Queens Room situated on the Upper and Quarter Decks respectively. The bands are also required to play in the two main restaurants for dancing during dinner, a comparatively recent, and popular, innovation.

In the Club Lido, always popular with the younger element, there is a top-grade disco-theque nightly with a live band playing here until the early hours. The popular Theatre Bar features a duo of piano player and girl vocalist who also doubles on the saxophone, while in the new Yacht Club Bar at aperitif time, a professional performs on the elegant glazed piano.

Turning to cabaret, the nightly shows — alternating between the two main lounges — feature classical concert artistes of international repute, male and female vocalists, comedians and comediennes, and specialist instrumentalists such as the Paraguayan harpist who performed on recent voyages. Often there are magicians or hypnotists, and currently a talented team of modern dancers which has certainly proved its popularity.

Increasingly popular are the lecture programmes, the lecturers being happy to offer their services free in return for the ride to or from New York. For this purpose usually three cabins are set aside permanently, and sometimes more if available. Lectures normally take place in the ship's theatre, where the latest films are also screened twice daily at 16.00hrs and 22.00hrs.

A professional ballroom dancing team travels with the ship, not only to perform as part of the daily show programme, but also to provide complimentary instruction in their art as qualified teachers, such popular sessions featuring frequently in the day's programme.

Ships like the QE2 have often been described somewhat tritely as 'floating hotels'. Yes they are, with the difference that in their case free entertainment is provided *in situ*, without the necessity of venturing forth to find (and pay) for it.

On this first day at sea, passengers have a choice at 10.45hrs of attending either the first of the lectures, or a computer seminar in the recently enlarged Computer Learning Centre. In the first case the subject of the lecture is graphology, the process of character judgement from handwriting, while the Computer Learning

Centre not only has become popular with enthusiasts but also with newcomers eager to try their hands under the expert direction of a professional lecturer in computer studies. Already some 20,000 previous passengers have 'graduated' in the sciences of home or office technology. Also at 10.45hrs, teenagers of 13 and over, meeting in the Teens Centre, are given a conducted tour of 'the world's greatest liner', while in the Grand Lounge the Social Directress tells her audience more about the Cunard company and its flagship. Simultaneously, for golfing enthusiasts, the ship's professional is giving coaching towards improving handicaps on the spacious sports area aft on the Upper Deck, a corpulent passenger fervently bemoaning a continuing habit to 'pull' the ball!

The always popular Mobile Tote follows, giving people the chance to bet on the mileage covered from the Cherbourg departure until noon today. The Mobile Tote Board is situated in the social staff centre, which, on the stroke of noon, receives from the Bridge the actual mileage steamed. The winner of the contest is the passenger whose guess falls nearest to the correct figure, and substantial sums of money may be won daily from this the longest established contest in the history of sea travel.

Food for Thought

Lunch is now upon us and it would be convenient to interrupt description of the entertainment programme to comment on the two principal Restaurants and the two Grill Rooms in the *QE2*.

For passengers eating in the Columbia Restaurant on the Quarter Deck forward and those qualified by the cost of their tickets to eat in either of the Grill Rooms, lunch begins at 12.30hrs, continuing until 14.00hrs, while there are two sittings in the Mauretania Restaurant situated on the Upper Deck — the first at noon and the second at 13.30hrs. Whether a passenger is seated in the Columbia or the Mauretania Restaurant is governed by the price of his or her cabin, while those seated in the Grill Rooms are travelling in the higher priced cabins in Groups AA to D. This is probably the remaining vestige of the old class system of the scheduled passenger liner, there being otherwise no firm barriers to any passenger as in the days of the *Queen* liners,

although as a rule people seated in the Mauretania Restaurant are quietly discouraged from using the bars of either Grill Room before meals. The elegant Columbia Restaurant underwent a facelift during the German refit, the new basic ambience being a dusky pink mingled with soft beige, grey and white accents. It extends over the entire breadth of the ship, full length plate-glass windows giving ample views of the sea or other sights. Mirrored sections of the bulkheads add cleverly to the general effect of spaciousness and a recently added improvement has been the addition of a dance floor for use during dinner.

The Mauretania Restaurant (alias 'Tables of the World' and before that the 'Britannia') has also undergone extensive improvement and refurbishment. Elegantly framed photographs of passenger life aboard the famous *Mauretania* of 1907, line the walls, the crowning feature being a glorious glass-encased model set on a plinth in a commanding position of the room. Passengers seem surprised to be told that the old four-stacker was just about half the size of *QE2* with but one funnel! There is no difference in culinary standards between the Columbia and Mauretania Restaurants, the latter giving excellent value for

money against the more modestly priced cabins dictating its usage, although it has the slight inconvenience for dictating two sittings to those unaccustomed to eating early.

For passengers travelling in the more expensive cabins categorised from AA to D, there are the two Grill Rooms. The larger of these, the Queen's Grill and adjoining reception lounge, is located on the Boat Deck forward. Here the decor is a soft white contrasting with black trimmings — smart and restful to the eye, although the room gives the impression of slight overcrowding at peak times.

Those discerning people who have known the *QE2* from her early days may well opt for the Princess Grill on the Quarter Deck port side, one of the most elegant rooms in the view of many. Here, however, seating is limited to 138, and it is thus restricted to use by passengers travelling in the deluxe accommodation under category D. Wine-coloured padded walls blend with the crown design of the carpeting, the whole effect enhanced by some exceptionally pleasing statu-

Above:
Focal point of the Queen's Room is the gold leaf-covered bust of Her Majesty Queen Elizabeth II.

ary set on plinths around the room. The Princess Grill is approached up a pretty spiral stairway from a small reception and aperitif area beneath.

With lunch behind them, passengers may be tempted to take a snooze in their rooms or in some quiet area of the ship, before resuming the day's entertainment, including a second lecture on the role of the author in an expanding society, delivered by a celebrated, award-winning name in writing. Alternatively there is an introductory session of gaming in the Casino at 15.00hrs, with complimentary chips, while at the same hour the ballroom dancing instructors begin a complimentary dance class in the Grand Lounge, where enthusiasts are welcome — with or without partners.

In the 'Golden Spa Door at Sea', a 30min workout focuses on abdominal muscle control under the supervision of experts, and then, at 16.30hrs a session of the ever-popular Bingo begins in the Queen's Room, supervised by members of the Cruise Director's staff. Meanwhile the afternoon film in the theatre has attracted admirers of Michael Caine starring in his latest role.

The Daily Programme leaflet has politely suggested formal dress to be worn this evening,

meaning that tuxedos and formal ladies' attire have been removed for pressing by the cabin staff in preparation for the first social event of the voyage, the Captain's cocktail party for those eating in the Columbia Restaurant and Grill Rooms. Undoubtedly the concessionaire hair stylists, Steiners, will also have had a busy time creating new hairdos for this event, which is scheduled to start promptly at 18.45hrs when the Master, in full Mess Uniform, receives his guests at the forward, starboard side entrance to the Queen's Room — many of them familiar faces from previous voyages. The social staff mingle among the guests, ensuring that they have a drink in their hand served by attentive waiters, and introducing them to various of the ship's Officers — all fully attired for the occasion — who must now be ready to answer a barrage of questions about the ship, whether they directly concern their departments or not.

The party continues for an hour, after which there are polite suggestions that the guests might care to move into dinner — tonight a gala one.

The Gala Dinner menu offers firstly a selection of *hors-d'oeuvres*, including Russian Malossol caviar served with chopped onion, egg and sour cream, following which there is a choice of three soups. The main courses offer the following:

● Roast American Prime Ribs of Beef with French Green Beans and Baked Potato in jacket garnished with Sour Cream and Chives; or
● Medallions of Veal served on Bell Pepper Stripes and Morels (an exotic form of mushroom shipped during the Cherbourg call), with Gorgonzola Cream; or
● Tender Breast of Chicken filled with a Mousse of Crabmeat, baked in the oven and served on a bed of Spinach with Sauce Newbourg.
● There is a selection of vegetables beyond those offered with the main dishes, and a green salad — tonight a *Caesar á la mode du Chef*.
● To round off the menu, desserts vary between a delicious Hazelnut Soufflé, fresh Strawberries with Whipped Cream, Raspberry Sherbert, and a selection of Ices. Throughout dinner the wine waiter and his assistants move from table to table taking orders for, and serving, wines of the diners' choice, or making recommendations when invited to.

Always available are Kosher menus, and a passenger may order any special dish of his choice off the menu, provided that he gives his table steward advance warning of the requirement. It is Cunard's proud boast that only in the rarest cases have passengers' requests been turned down. On one of the ship's world cruises she numbered among her wealthier clientele a London butcher possessed of a strong and unvarying taste for Shepherd's Pie. It need hardly be said that the Chefs obliged with an interesting and delicious variety of ways to serve this otherwise unassuming dish.

To enliven the proceedings, one of the two dance bands swings into the nostalgic sounds of Berlin, Porter, Rodgers, Coward and others, encouraging diners to take to the floor between courses. The scene is one of festive elegance, and while certain seasoned travellers may hark back to the golden years of the *Queen* ships, the *Liberte*, and the *United States*, complaining that today's style in no way compares with them, one wonders if these people might not reassess such views if suddenly transported back in time to one of these old ladies. What would they say for a start at having to fare without the many more modern conveniences of today's liners? And while menus today may not offer the same range of choice, there is no doubting the quality of the dishes they offer. After the meal the passengers have enjoyed this evening, some of them may well be glad of a visit to the 'Golden Spa Door at Sea' on the morrow!

After dinner, passengers spread themselves around the areas of entertainment to enjoy coffee with liqueurs, Cognac or vintage Port wine, dancing in either of the main rooms and watching the cabaret shows. This evening there is a display by the chique modern dancers in the Queen's Room, and an act by the ballroom team in the Grand Lounge. Many younger passengers are already in the Club Lido, working off their dinners by dancing the night away to the latest sounds disco.

Keen gamblers or those seeking a modest flutter at the tables or banks of slot machines visit the Players Club Casino to attend the second session of gaming at 21.30hrs, keeping the croupiers coolly and dexterously busy, while others are in the theatre by this time to view the second film presentation of the day.

On finally retiring, passengers may reflect that the remainder of the voyage — just three whole days — is likely to vanish all too quickly, given the degree of activity. Before succumbing to sleep, they should remember to retard watches or clocks so as to ensure keeping step with the ship and eventually coinciding with local time on their New York arrival — currently five hours behind British Summer Time.

Power Behind the Throne

Having described the activities of the Deck Dept and its Officers, it is now time to turn to the other area of major importance, the ship's main engines.

Given full rein it would be possible to devote an entire book to the subject of the *QE2's* new propulsion plant, such is its sophistication and complexity. When in November 1986, she proceeded to the yard of Lloyd Werft in Bremerhaven for a six-month refit, the prime object of the exercise was the removal of her ageing turbine plant, and its replacement by a new diesel electric system. The difference between the latter and the more familiar method of diesel motor propulsion is that in the one, power is transmitted electrically, while mechanically in the other.

At its simplest, the *QE2* today is equipped with nine diesel engines manufactured by MAN-Burmeister & Wain both celebrated names in the history of motor propulsion at sea. Attached to each of these engines is a generator supplied by the equally prestigious name of GEC. For purposes of description, the nine combined units may be referred to as generators that provide the electrical power to a pair of main propulsive motors — also of GEC make — as well as for domestic services and others throughout the ship. In itself this is somewhat of a novelty, older ships having been equipped with different systems for each purpose. However, the really big novelty stems from the fact that the entire system is computer controlled, not only shutting down or activating the generators automatically according to power requirement, but also monitoring the proper functioning of accompanying essentials such as the lubricating oil pumps and activating alternatives in the event of failure.

The two main motors are linked, through a main thrust, to twin propeller shafts lying along the customary tunnels — port and starboard — linking eventually to tailshafts that pass through glands in the ship's shell and out to the twin propellers. The latter are of the variable-pitch design, meaning that the blades may be angled to a number of positions, controlling the speed of the ship irrespective of shaft revolutions. For example we see that in Combinator Mode, with shafts turning at 72rpm, there is no actual propulsion so long as the propellers remain at Zero Pitch.

Conversion of the machinery clearly involved massive rearrangement of the available spaces, including, of course, the herculean task of lifting out the old turbines and the three huge boilers that provided the steam for them. Moreover, the greater number of exhaust uptakes required by the new system, necessitated the fitting of a distinctly more robust funnel in which to carry them — a distinct improvement in the eyes of many traditionalists.

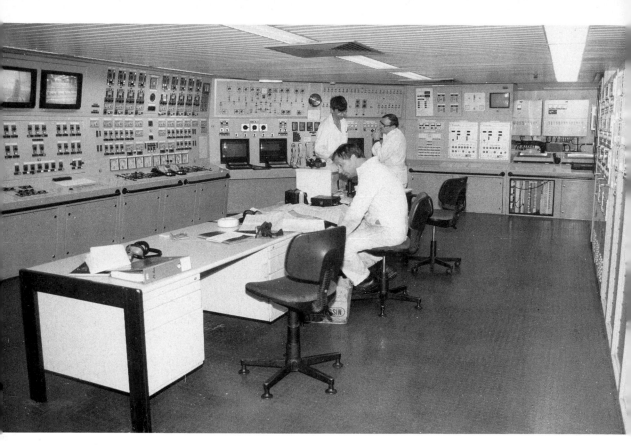

Whereas the ship's earlier machinery occupied just two compartments — one housing the boilers the other the turbines — today there are four compartments within the same area. The first most forward compartment is the ECR (Engine Control Room), the control centre for the entire generator plant. Moving aft, the second compartment contains four of the nine main engines (Alpha, Bravo, Charlie and Delta) and is thus the 'Forward Machinery Space'. The third compartment is the 'Aft Machinery Space' containing the five remaining engines (Echo, Foxtrot, Golf, Hotel and India). The fourth compartment is the 'Propulsion Motor Room' and contains both GEC electric propulsion motors plus a plethora of air-vent trunking necessary to provide air cooling to the very large motors.

The propulsion system of the QE2 can be split up into two parts: the first taking care of the electric power generation and distribution, and the other part providing and controlling thrust to the propellers and maintaining ship speed.

The equipment is distributed throughout in a number of compartments so that loss of a switchboard room or engine room will not result in a total loss of propulsion power nor of the supply to the vessel as a whole.

As previously mentioned, the power generation is by nine MAN-B&W turbocharged marine diesel engines driving nine GEC synchronous, brushless, ac generators, rated 10,500kW at 400rpm, with four gensets in the forward engine room and five gensets in the aft engine room. The operating voltage for the propulsion system is 10,000V at 60Hz frequency, ie it is a constant voltage/frequency system. The GEC high voltage switchboard is divided into two main sections, with all necessary circuit breakers, protection relays, synchronising equipment and sequencing relays. A changeover panel enables either converter to be used with either propulsion motor. Two transformers rated 11MVa, 10/3.3kV supply power to the general ship service distribution system.

The two LIPS controllable pitch propellers are each driven by a GEC electric motor. The propulsion motors — salient pole synchronous ac motors, rated 44,000kW at 144rpm — are designed for variable frequency starting using GEC synchro-converters, rated 11,000kW at 144rpm. At low shaft speed of 72rpm the output of the converters is restricted to 5,500kW.

The propulsion motors run normally at a constant synchronous speed of 144rpm corresponding to 60Hz. At low ship speeds below

Above left:
The Engine Control Room (ECR).

Above:
A view across the 'tops' of engines 'Alpha', 'Bravo', 'Charlie' and 'Delta' in the Forward Machinery Space.

Right:
The port propulsion motor showing the air-cooling fan motors in the propulsion motor room.

approximately 18kt they are operated at a speed varying between 72 and 144rpm by means of the synchro-converters. Cruising up to 17kt is done preferably at a constant propeller speed of 72rpm.

Operation of the entire system is by fully automated electronic governors, and the system provides for a number of operating modes.

● *Harbour Mode*
With ship moored alongside and the propulsion motors shut down, this allows ideally for just one generator (plus a second on warm standby) to be

Above:
The port propeller shaft.

Left:
The main engine controls in the ECR.

Above right:
Routine maintenance on one of the nine main engine turbochargers.

Right:
Second Engineer John Mills pictured at the Power Management Computer controls.

running on load to provide power to all basic ship's services.

● *Ready To Sail Mode*

Where a further three or four engines are running on load ready for propulsion motor-start and propeller rotation.

● *Combinator Mode*

At either 72rpm (giving speeds of up to 18kt) or 144rpm (speeds of 20kt plus).

● *Free Sailing Mode*

For when the vessel is clear of manoeuvring waters and both motors are at 144rpm with a minimum of five engines on load. A 'soft loading' programme then allows for further engines to be started and loaded-up until required speed is attained, or a maximum of nine engines are on full load and vessel is at full speed.

The normal service speed of the *QE2* is 28½kt, but with appreciable margin in hand for maintaining schedules if necessary. Thus we see from Lloyd Werft's records on trial speed performance in April 1987 that maximum speed ahead was 34.6kt which, with adjustment for adverse tide, netted back to 33.8kt. Promptly there was public speculation as to whether Cunard might make an attempt to recover the once coveted Blue Riband of the Atlantic held to this day by the now mothballed *United States*. As, however, this great American ship wrested the trophy from *Queen Mary* at an average speed at least 2kt in excess of *QE2's* best on trials, this would seem to be a pointless and strainful exercise. Why not leave the American lady her laurels, or any further attempts to Mr Richard Branson?

The huge and complicated task of re-engining the *QE2* with a system so different from the original must rank as one of the outstanding achievements of today and those concerned should feel justifiably proud of it, despite early and persistent teething troubles following the ship's redelivery.

In charge of this complexity of new technology is the personage of the Chief Engineer, the 'Chief' as he is referred to in most ships, assisted in *QE2* by no less than 11 assistants reducing in rank, and up to six electrical engineers — especially vital one would imagine in a system so reliant on electrical power.

Should it be imagined that the Chief is a man who rarely sees the light of day, remaining deep in his throbbing domain, forever clad in a boiler suit, this would be entirely wrong. He must play his full role in the daily socialising, hosting his own cocktail parties along with other senior colleagues, ready to answer innumerable queries about 'his' machinery.

The Voyage — Day 2

The second day at sea dawns fine and clear, yesterday's cloud having dispersed during the night. The ship steams westward at 28kt, a light sou'westerly breeze rippling the now blue water. Thus far the North Atlantic has behaved itself and there is nothing to suppose from the weather forecasts that there will be any real change for the rest of the voyage.

It is warm enough to expect that later in the morning the decks will be popular with sunbathers and that the swimming pools on the two lido decks will be in full use; the high grade polycarbonate roof panels of the Magrodome draw aside, opening the Quarter Deck pool to sun and air. The Magrodome was a new addition during her 1983 refit in Germany, and while it has slightly marred the external, tiered symmetry of the ship aft, nobody could doubt its popularity in more breezy conditions than today's.

The day is Sunday and at 08.30hrs Holy Mass is celebrated in the theatre by a Roman Catholic Monsignor, while at 11.15hrs — also in the theatre — an interdenominational service is conducted by the Master of the ship.

Thereafter a programme as comprehensive as that of the previous day gets into its stride, including a lecture on the subject of the former *Queen* liners by a leading marine historian, having been born and bred near the waterfront of Hoboken, New Jersey, across the Hudson from the Manhattan Piers — an avid watcher of ships from early boyhood. Today there are two further

Below:
The Safety Control Room is hidden away on No 2 Deck and is the control centre for all safety-related matters from fire alarm and sprinkler control panels to oil fuel transfers and sea water ballast control.

lectures, the first questioning whether nuclear weaponry is here to stay, and the other providing a peep into book publishing by the celebrated author/lecturer of the previous day. There is a further session in the ever-popular computer room, a repeat of the complimentary dancing class in the Grand Lounge, and at 17.00hrs a special show — again in the Grand Lounge — the 'American Dance Machine'. As expected, many of the passengers have stripped down to swimwear, young men drooling over some of the deeply-tanned girls in bikinis, while waiters move constantly among them with offers of light refreshments. Soon it is time to don the towelling wraps provided by Cunard to return to cabins and prepare for dinner. Although today's programme has suggested a relaxation from formal wear, this does not imply appearance in the dining rooms without jackets, and the ladies seem to look as smart as they did at the previous evening's Gala Dinner. Nor does this 'relaxation' imply the slightest lowering in the quality of the food itself. The mood is as festive as ever while passengers sample yet another of the *QE2's* menus, others enjoying the special dishes they have ordered previously.

Afterwards, there is a special concert at 21.30hrs in the theatre by a professional classical pianist who performs the 'Warsaw Concerto', the 'Minute' Waltz, and Rachmaninov's 18 variations before switching to a lighter note with 'The wonderful world of Richard Rodgers'. Again there is dancing in both main lounges interspersed with floor shows, while at 22.00hrs the second film of the day features Jack Nicholson and Cher in a strange story of modern witchery — The Witches of Eastwick.

It should be said that before both lunch and dinner today there have been a number of cocktail parties in the quarters of the senior Officers from the Master and Staff Captain

Queen Elizabeth 2   *Cunard Line*

CAPTAIN ROBIN A. WOODALL R.D. R.N.R.

requests the pleasure of your company

for cocktails in his quarters

At _____ *On* _____

Your Steward will direct you

downwards, guests having been predetermined by the social staff on discussion with the officers concerned. The appearance of an invitation under the cabin door is much coveted by certain of the passengers who may feel distinctly slighted if the entire voyage passes without sign of the magic envelope on the bedroom carpet! At times some of the guests at these parties are inveterate 'name droppers', and the story is told of a Cunard Master's mystification over one loud lady's incessant references to 'Liz and Phil'. Finally the penny dropped. Turning to a rather quieter lady on his other side, he whispered 'I believe she is referring to our Head of State and her husband'!

As the second day draws to its close, passengers retire to retard watches once again, reflecting that they have now reached the halfway point. There are but two days left of this remarkable cocooned existence away from it all before the frenzy and pace of city existence devours them once more.

A Hotel Afloat

Clearly, a ship, without engine power or navigational capabilities is not a ship at all. Similarly a passenger liner without any manner of hotel services would be just a ship. *QE2* embodies the best of both worlds by providing five star-plus hotel services aboard a ship, with engine and navigational capabilities second to none.

The head of the Hotel Dept is the Hotel Manager who rules a domain so large that each division within that domain has a manager who is directly answerable to the Hotel Manager.

● *The Kitchens*

Under the direction of an Executive Chef with upwards of 100 assistants beneath him, clearly the vital importance of this section alone cannot be underestimated — not only in terms of providing the best food, but also in the maintenance of cleanliness and high standards of hygiene. The rules of the US Public Health Service are especially stringent and the ship's staff may expect snap inspections from its officers at any time — without prior warning. Percentage points are awarded to the ship in a number of areas, not the least being the kitchens, the state of the equipment therein and above all the handling of food by individuals. If a ship fails to achieve the prescribed standards, there is prompt notification to such effect, a severe warning given and the promise that the Inspector will return in a matter of weeks to satisfy himself that his previous directions have been adequately carried out. If at that point the ship still fails to meet standards she is liable to be removed from

DECK PLANS

Signal Deck, Sports Deck, Boat Deck,
Upper Deck and Quarter Deck are not to scale.

UPPER DECK

BOAT DECK

SIGNAL DECK

SPORTS DECK

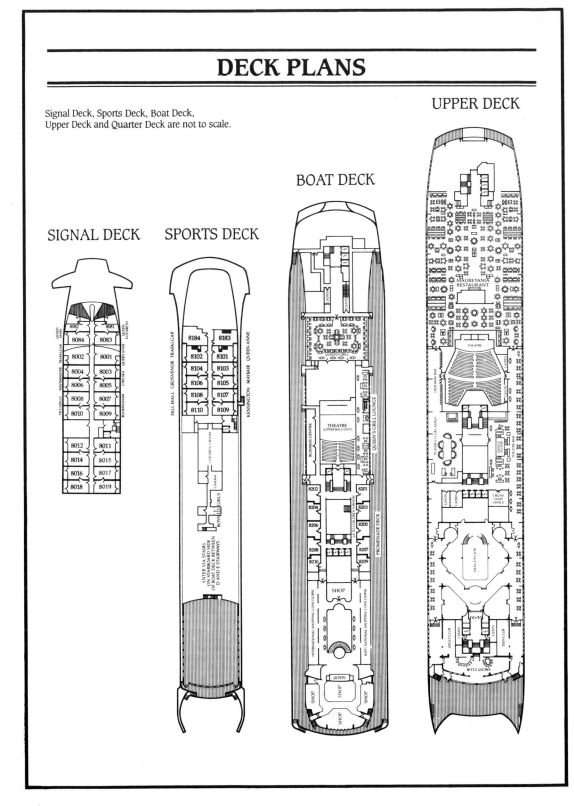

Above:
The main kitchen takes a breather between meals.

Below:
On the 'Front Line': the Purser's Office front desk at No 2 Deck F stairway.

Above:
Back behind the 'Front': the Purser's staff are seen hard at work in the inner sanctum.

service with all that this implies in the loss of revenue and adverse press comment.

Again, a serious view is taken if a ship arrives at the end of a voyage, reporting a number of cases of sickness or diarrhoea among passengers or crew. In that event no stone will be unturned by the inspectors to find the cause of the epidemic, or the individual carrying or perpetrating the infection, often leading to further delay and hounding by the media. Indeed the Health Authority itself will make no attempt to conceal such an event in the general desire for immediate improvement. Inevitably inspectors are often disliked — even feared — but they are performing a very vital role and scarcely look for popularity in the process.

● *The Bars and Stores*
These are under the control of the Food and Beverage Manager.

● *The Purser's Office*
Under the direction of the Purser himself, whose staff in the large office on No 2 Deck is constantly available for administering to passengers' needs, often handling complaints in a variety of forms — genuine or trivial. No matter how high the standards, there is invariably a hard core of habitual grousers, who complain on the slightest pretext and invent fault even where it doesn't exist. With these people the Purser and his staff must be monuments to patience, curbing any human desire to let fly verbally against often severe goading.

There is the classic story of one young Purser's assistant, an English girl, working in another of the New York-based cruise ships. One fine afternoon, with the ship steaming midway between the Ambrose Light and Hamilton, Bermuda, the girl answered a call from one of the cabins.

'Hear me good', said a grating female voice, 'I have to leave this ship, and leave it now'!

Above:

QE2's onboard Printshop which is responsible for all printing requirements from menus and Daily Programmes to Cocktail Party invitation cards.

Curbing her astonishment, the girl replied politely that this might pose problems, the ship being in mid-ocean. Immediately she was reviled in a torrent of four-letter abuse, told not to be impertinent and asked why she spoke 'such funny English' anyway!

'For God's sake', the voice continued, 'haven't you people ever heard of helicopters?'

Then she demanded that one should be called for immediately and at the owners' expense. At that point the girl gave up, handing the receiver to the Purser himself. It is not on record what he said to the lady, but at Hamilton she left the ship by suitable mutual arrangement, probably meaning that she was refunded her entire passage money....

There are many stories related by the Purser's staff regarding ridiculously inane questions. The more well-known of these are:

'What time does the Midnight Buffet start?'

'Do these stairs go up?'

'Are the swimming pools fresh or salt water?' — 'Salt water Madam!' — 'No wonder they're so rough!'

And finally: 'How many fjords to the dollar?'

Further sections within the Hotel Division are:

- *The Restaurants and Grill Rooms* each with its own manager and waiting staff.
- *The Passenger Cabins* and all cabin staff under the Accommodation Services Manager.
- The very considerable laundry and cleaning facilities aboard the ship.
- *Food and Dry Stores* Today under computerised control so that at the pressing of a key, it may be shown which items are running low and require replacement.
- *The Cruise Director and his Staff* Importantly responsible for the passengers' pleasure and entertainment. Beneath him is the Entertainments Manager plus a Social Director and staff, responsible for arranging and co-ordinating all social affairs aboard, such as the Officers' cocktail parties and the issuing of printed invitations for same.
- *The Ship's Hospital and Medical Staff* Here there is a Senior Medical Officer, signed on ship's Articles, wearing the colour red between the three full rings on his uniform sleeves. Assisting him is a second MO — also articled — and three Nursing Sisters, all qualified from the Royal College of Nursing, and one or two as Midwives as well! There are 20 hospital beds equally divided between male and female sections, as well as a fully-equipped Operating Theatre in the event of emergency, with four male assistants. As earlier stated, Medical Consultants are employed in Southampton to render advice to Cunard on the stocks of medicines and drugs that need to be carried in the ship at all times, there being a qualified Pharmacist in the Medical

Below:

The Hospital Dispensary.

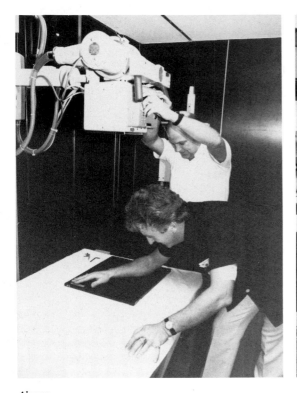

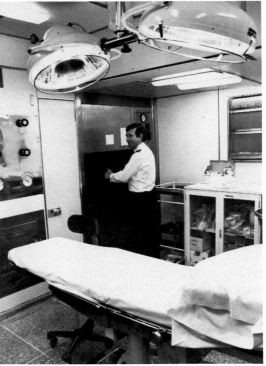

Above:
'Hold still, sir. *This won't hurt a bit!'* even an X-ray is available in mid-ocean!

Above:
The Operating Theatre: thankfully, rarely used.

Below:
'*Now, this won't hurt a bit!'* One of the three Nursing Sisters employed aboard *QE2* ensures any treatment required by either passengers or crew is carried out swiftly and efficiently.

Centre for dispensing them as needed on doctor's prescription. On more extended cruises, a Dentist is also carried.

● *The Public Rooms Manager and his Staff*
They are responsible for the constant good appearance and smooth working of all public rooms in the ship. In these the Manager supervises all staff in the service of drinks and light refreshments, as well as controlling the 'gang' of some 200 Philipinos, whose duty it is to keep the rooms cleaned and tidied.

● *The Security Team*
Such is the vast area embracing Hotel Services numbering a staff of nearly 800 men and women, but there are other important sections as well. Excepting the one major bomb scare of 1972, and the subsequent uncovering of an arms cache destined for the IRA, the *QE2* appears to have remained clear of troubles of this frightening kind — possibly due in no small measure to the presence aboard of a thoroughly alert security team, which is responsible officially to the Master of the ship, although in this case he has delegated the duty to his Staff Captain. The Chief Security Officer is a two-and-a-half ringer, usually recruited from the Army or the RN as Warrant Officer or Petty Officer respectively —

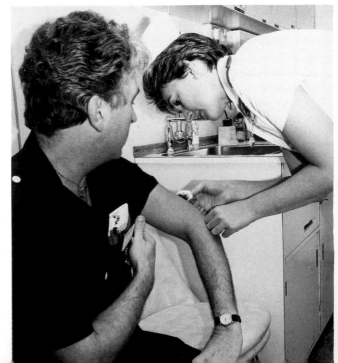

fully trained in the handling of explosive and bomb disposal. Beneath him are his senior security Petty Officers performing as gangway guards when in port, as well as carrying out the extensive clock patrols throughout the ship. In order to avoid disturbing passengers unnecess-

arily, the security officers go about their business in low profile, but the former may be comforted to know of this ever-vigilant team in their midst.

Crew members aboard *QE2* fall broadly into two distinct categories: Hotel staff and non-Hotel staff, the latter being primarily UK-resident and employed through Cunard's offices in Southampton. The majority of Hotel staff (up to 480 in total) are employed through a manning agency called 'Columbia Ship Management'. This agency is Cyprus-based and is responsible for the manning of over 120 ships worldwide. Only four of these ships are passenger vessels and *QE2* is the only British ship.

A CSM representative sails aboard *QE2* at all times and acts as a local Personnel Manager for CSM employees in all matters, from pay and leave to discipline and travel vouchers. The representative is hotel-trained and invariably female.

The Radio Room

When the radio installation on *QE2* was designed back in 1968 by the International Marine Radio Company (IMR Co) it was envisaged that a total of nine operating staff would be employed on board at any one time. This, however, was not to be the case and the vessel started life with six staff, Chief, First, Technical and three Watchkeeping officers. Over the years, this number has dwindled to a total of three officers and two assistants handling the telephone calls.

'Autospec' telex equipment was placed on board in 1968 but this was a very hit-and-miss affair and has been superseded by 'Sitor', a much improved Marconi System. Two units are carried at this time.

Satellite was in its infancy in the late 1960s and *QE2* carried the first Comsat test rig in 1972 and it proved a success. In 1976 the first commercial installation Comsat Terminal was placed on board and this ran quite happily until 1987 when an STC Mascot installation was purchased and improved the speed of communication. In July 1989 a four-channel Magnavox installation was provided and this gives credit card convenience and direct cabin-to-shore dialling.

The ship's newspaper is downloaded by satellite from the Oceansat News Offices in Fort Lauderdale in a total of around 8min and this provides eight pages of news, sport and finance. In the early days, two systems were utilised — Plessey and Piccolo — and eight pages were received daily from the offices of the *Daily Telegraph* in London, but this took anything from 2-8hr, depending upon reception conditions.

Satellite also provides TV coverage from a choice of many satellites, but the quality varies according to the size of footprint (coverage). Pictures are obtained on three days of a five-day Atlantic crossing.

Below:
First Radio Officer Chris Connerty amid the galaxy of receivers and transmitters that make up a modern Radio Room.

Much of the ship's telex traffic is sent and received by satellite with worldwide direct dialling at our fingertips.

Should they ever be required, QE2 has two fixed lifeboat radio installations giving Morse coverage on 500kHz and 8MHz, and voice coverage on 2MHz. In addition, we also carry two hand portables giving the same facilities as the fixed installations. In the transmitter room there is also a complete battery-powered emergency installation should the need arise.

Computers are in the Radio Room to stay and much of the ship's business is carried out using a duplex high speed data transmission system linking the ship to Cunard's main offices in New York, Southampton, Liverpool, Hamburg and Fort Lauderdale. What would have taken an hour to transmit by telex now takes about 3min on this 'Marinet' data system.

QE2 is now equipped with a 'Fax' machine which is becoming increasingly popular with both ship managers and passengers. Documents may be transmitted by either satellite or landline when the ship is in port.

Occasionally it is necessary to sit down and take weather reports, ice broadcasts and general warnings by Morse code but all this is changing rapidly and the majority of such information is received by FEC telex these days, thus releasing the Radio Officer for other duties.

Although the staff are kept very busy, it can be seen why, due to automation, direct dialling, etc, the original concept of nine officers has now been so drastically reduced to three. The Nixdorf automatic telephone exchange, installed in 1987, cut out the need for five telephone staff and all phone traffic is handled by the Radio staff.

Crew Facilities

In a close community such as that of QE2, crew recreation is of paramount importance and this is predominantly the responsibility of the Staff Captain. At the 1987 refit in Germany, opportunity was taken to improve the crew facilities aboard the ship through substantial investment in new rooms and attractive decor. For a start all 460 of the ratings' cabins were generally overhauled and modernised in a number of cases, while the messing area forward on No 1 Deck was completely renewed. The Mess itself, Servery, Recreation Room, Shop, Library, Barber's Shop, Gymnasium, Club Room and Crew Lounge were all refurbished and redecorated in pleasant contemporary style, new TV and video equipment being provided in several cases. One room is given over for the exclusive use of female staff, another for non-drinkers, and a third offering quiet conditions for reading and writing.

The policy aboard lies towards minimising the consumption of alcohol among the crew and there are periodic lectures to this end by the Medical Officers and others, warning of the dangers of over-indulgence. Having said this, the ratings have their own bar, where beer and soft drinks are served — and spirits only in the evening. Today, crew shows are more frequent — about twice a month — when either the professionals travelling with the ship will give a performance, or members of the crew itself produce their own shows — many of them uproariously funny.

Outside deck areas are set aside for fresh air and sun-bathing, including passenger areas at certain times, though the customers, of course, must enjoy precedence at all times.

The greatest criticism of the old Queen Mary and her slightly newer running mate, Queen Elizabeth to a lesser extent, related to their very poor facilities provided for ratings, but these bad days are long past. Crew facilities aboard QE2 bear no relation to those of the late 1930s or even the postwar period.

For the 120 or so officer personnel there is a wardroom on the Boat Deck forward, sub-divided into bar and restaurant areas, the former offering TV, video, darts and other such facilities, while at the same level there is also a messroom for the professional entertainers and the ship's social staff, offering similar facilities.

Public Rooms

Of the numerous public rooms and areas aboard QE2, the restaurants and grill rooms have already been described in some detail, and now we should turn to the other main areas of interest.

Many who have experienced travel by her, in earlier years, will have opted for the Queen's Room on the Quarter Deck aft as the most stylish, elegant and restful room in the ship. This was the original creation of the distinguished decor consultant David Hicks and his motif here was a shade of off-white, with chairs and sofas upholstered in a light fawn, set off here and there by colourful touches and some especially graceful swung columns sweeping upwards to an unusual deckhead arrangement. Today the basic motif survives, but at the 1987 refit the chairs and sofas which had blended so well with the general effect, were replaced by somewhat ponderous, low-backed items — metal framed — in a chocolate brown, leather-style of material that sadly seems to have robbed the room of some of its original style, though inevitably there are those who prefer the new to the old.

Easily the most spectacular room in the ship today is the Grand Lounge on the Upper Deck — originally known as the Double Down Room for offering two seating levels, and the creation of John Bannenberg, a strong exponent of the 1960s styles. Until the 1987 refit the room had two levels, a slightly awkward spiral staircase leading downwards to the low level from an encircling balcony. Today the balcony forms a new and stylish shopping arcade while the old spiral stairway has been replaced by a horseshoe-style affair that flanks the bandstand and stage at the forward end of the room. At the same time the lounge itself has been ingeniously terraced for better viewing of the stage and dance floor, while it is noticeable that many casual onlookers of the nightly shows prefer to view the performances from the rail of the shopping balcony above. At the refit, the walls of the Grand Lounge were faced with bird's-eye maple and a white laminate, while the hundreds of red and blue-covered chairs are grouped around small glass tables. Here again the decor is unlikely to please everybody, but unquestionably this is an eye-catching room and a distinct improvement on the somewhat dated original.

In the original Double Down Room at its after end was the Double Down Bar — never greatly used. At the last refit this was converted into the new Yacht Bar, which has already proved its popularity as a centre for evening aperitifs. The maritime effect here is enhanced by a wave-shaped deckhead, models of yachts and spectacular photographic posters. A further highlight of this room is the glazed piano with drink rail and bar stools stretched around it, allowing for users to make their requests to the performer at relatively close quarters. Aficionados of the original QE2 are relieved to find that the exceptionally elegant Midships Bar on the Quarter Deck, starboard side, has remained much as it was, the basic effect still being a relaxing deep green against darker walls. This continues to be a highly popular gathering spot before dinner in the nearby Columbia Restaurant.

The Club Lido is located aft of the Queen's Room, leading directly to the Magrodome and upper swimming pool. This whole area was the subject of conversion at the 1983 refit in Germany and has certainly proved its popularity since. There are large, glass sliding doors to divide the Club Lido itself and the area of the swimming pool-cum-Magrodome. In the evenings the glazed dance floor is illuminated, encouraging passengers to work off their dinners to the beat of the discotheque and later the Caribbean six-piece.

The Teen Centre lies next to the Grand Lounge at its after end, adjacent on the starboard side to the main stairway. Here we find a jumbo-sized television set, a variety of video games, a music complex and a small dance floor. The motif is similar to that of the Yacht Bar — essentially maritime, with innovative wall panels and deckhead. There is little doubt of the popularity of this room — not only with the young, but adults also — especially since this is the centre for table tennis, where daily contests are arranged between passengers and ship's staff. Exactly measuring the Teen Centre on the port side is the adult equivalent fitted with a reading corner, card tables and shuffleboard. Lying aft of the Yacht Club Bar is the principal outdoor sporting area equipped with a putting green, two shuffleboard pitches, and a multi-functional central area for basketball, badminton, paddle tennis and punchball, not forgetting the golf driving range.

At the last refit in 1987, the swimming pool on No 1 Deck lido aft was renewed as was the surrounding teak deck. Also added was a children's paddling pool and two whirlpools, along with new deck chairs and sun-shaded tables.

First impressions are invariably important and to this end, the main lobby on No 2 Deck was also given a new facelift in 1987. Redecorated and re-upholstered in a motif of white and blue, it also has a piano in the central well, played during embarkation.

The much-enlarged shopping areas are a natural attraction in the QE2, comprising not only the original International Shopping Concourse on the Boat Deck starboard, but also the newly-converted balcony area encircling the Grand Lounge. Here we find such international names as Louis Ferraud, Vuitton, Christian Dior, H. Stern, Gucci, Dunhill and others. The Harrods shop is situated separately on No 1 Deck 'D' stair — no more, however, than an up-market gift shop offering a variety of attractive goods.

The important areas occupied by the three kitchens were also largely renovated at the 1987 refit, great thought being given to layout and equipment in consideration of the stringent standards set by United States Public Health Service and the World Health Organisation. Snap visits by Inspectors on the US seaboard should no longer be quite the fearsome occasions of the past, given, of course, a modicum of sweet reason in the attitudes of the Inspectors themselves.

Leaving the machinery replacement aside, the degree of renovation and refurbishment carried out in the passenger areas at recent refits, amply lends weight to the claim that within her basic shell, superstructure and deck arrangement, the QE2 has become virtually a 'new' ship — well able to stand up to all-comers in terms of competition. To her many historic supporters who complain that Cunard seems unable to resist the temptation towards 'messing about' with her accommodation, one might apply a gentle reminder that if her owners turned the Nelson eye to maintaining step with constantly-changing tastes, they might soon find themselves out of business!

Passenger Cabins

No description of the accommodation would be complete without reference to the passenger cabins spread throughout the ship from the Signal Deck down to No 5 Deck. These are categorised in varying price levels ranging from AA down to M, to suit a spread of pockets.

Beginning at the lower end are those rooms in the J, K, L and M Groups, varying in rates according to their deck level (to some extent) and to whether they are inside or outside cabins. Even the lowest rated among these, the Ms, offer functional comfort with fitted carpeting, adequate wardrobe and drawer spaces, albeit that one of the twin beds is at the upper level and that none of these categories is equipped with private baths as such. But unlike the North Atlantic ships of the past, such rooms are less restricted to the lower levels, being spread over Nos 1, 2, 3, 4 and 5 Decks.

Moving up the scale are the 'I' rated rooms, limited to No 4 Deck — all outsiders and with baths en suite. While located at a comparatively low level, these cabins offer excellent value for being rated at comparatively modest fares. Rooms in the G and H categories, located on Nos 1, 2 and 3 Decks — again all outsiders with private bath — are also of good value at some $800 in excess of the 'I' category, while at this point we enter the 'deluxe' range of rooms in the E and F categories located on Nos 1, 2 and 3 Decks, the term deluxe actually belying their comparatively modest rating in relation to the immediately lower category.

Now we come to the spread of ultra deluxe accommodation in categories B, C and D, situated between Nos 1, 2, 3 and the Sports and Boat Decks. In price these range between $5,504 for the best in the B category and $4,300 for those in category D, and there is no doubting their attractiveness throughout the range.

Beyond the ultra deluxe we reach the luxury class of attractive balconied rooms in the AA and A categories, situated on the Signal and Sports Decks between Bridge and funnel. The majority of these were added shortly following Cunard's acquisition by Trafalgar House and there has been no doubt of their popularity ever since. It should be said here that the figures quoted are those roughly applying to the 'Super Thrift', Air/Sea one way voyages and 'Thrift Excursion' levels for the 1990 season.

We come finally to the realms of millionaire travel — the beautiful suites located on the Signal Deck in the vicinity of the AA rooms. These offer two choices — either the Queen Mary/Queen Elizabeth split level apartments at $8,100, or the Trafalgar/Queen Anne Duplex suites at just over $6,900 on 1990 fare structures or the newly refurbished Midships Suite at $14,000. At these price levels, the cost of this accommodation for the full 'Around the World' (New York to New York) World Cruise in 1991 may be left to the imagination!

For those travelling alone there is a whole series of single rooms beginning at the lowest XE category — all inside rooms without bath — on Nos 2, 3, 4 and 5 Decks. These are followed by the WD cabins spread between the same levels, but all outside (without bath), and then by the VCs, consisting of inside rooms but slightly more costly than the WDs for being at a generally higher level in the ship. Category UB deluxe comprises outside single rooms with private baths located between Nos 1, 2, 3 and the Boat Deck, and finally the top category in singles is that of UA — all outside rooms with bath, described as ultra deluxe — located on Nos 1, 2 and the Boat Decks.

All passengers accommodated in the suites and the twin-berthed categories AA to C inclusive, are seated in the Queen's Grill, those under D in the Princess Grill, while categories E to H inclusive are allocated to the Columbia Restaurant, and I down to M to the Mauretania Restaurant.

Of the singles, category UA is seated in the Queen's Grill, UB and VC in the Columbia, and WD/XE in the Mauretania Restaurant.

Every passenger cabin has a telephone as part of a completely new system installed in 1987. The computer-supported exchange unit in the ship enables passengers to make telephone calls world-wide directly from their cabins at any time, while there is also, of course, an internal hotel circuit for use throughout the ship. Part of the system is the automatic wake-up service. By pressing the wake-up button before retiring and indicating the desired rousing time, the passenger is awakened by a cheerful voice: 'Good morning, this is your wake-up time . . . it is exactly 7.30am!'

There are operators among the cruise industry — particularly those using converted ships — who maintain that cabin quality is of lesser importance given adequacy of the Public Rooms, the outside Sports Areas and the high degree of entertainment activity or shore tours during the day. While this might be digestible in the short itineraries of seven days or less, it would never do in the QE2 or other ships employed on longer distances and attracting a clientele more demanding in its standards.

The Voyage — Days 3 and 4: Arrival New York

It is past 23.00hrs on the night of Tuesday, the last day of the westbound voyage. Many passengers have retired in readiness for the early disembarkation the following morning, but others — the intrepid livers of life — are determined to savour every last minute of the QE2 experience, intent on seeing the last night out and viewing the New York arrival. The Club Lido is doing roaring business to the discotheque and pop group, while that other popular spot in the late evening, the Theatre Bar, is also crowded.

In response to a request in today's Programme, passengers have packed all but their overnight bags, the bedroom staff having removed their main items to stack it in the alleyways, ready for carrying to the gangways on arrival. The North Atlantic on this voyage has continued to behave itself apart from intermittent fog banks encountered off Newfoundland, which kept the Master on the Bridge for several hours on end the previous evening and night. The first landfall with the United States, the flashing Nantucket Light, has already been passed and those passengers who saw it have realised wistfully that their voyage is all but over, with the great ship now on the last leg leading directly to the Ambrose Light where she is due to arrive dead on schedule at 04.00hrs. ETA messages to this effect have been sent to the New York Office, and barring any last-minute delay, the Master can now expect to maintain roughly the following timing:

- *04.00hrs* Arrival Ambrose.
- *04.15hrs* Pilot aboard.
- *05.30hrs* Passing beneath the Verazzano Bridge, spanning the narrows at the entrance to New York Harbour.
- *06.10hrs* Statue of Liberty abeam on port side.
- *06.25hrs* The Battery, southernmost tip of Manhattan Island abeam to starboard.
- *06.45hrs* Off the passenger terminal at West 49th Street.

Weather being good and other traffic light, the Master has left the Bridge after his nightly visit, leaving instructions in his order book to be called when the ship reaches a position 10 miles off Ambrose. The First and Second Officers of the 8-12 Watch are near to handing over to their successors on the 12-4, likewise the Coxswain and his assistant. Down below the midnight revellers are hard at it, and there are likely to be some throbbing heads in the morning! The night is warm and sultry, a portent of the sweltering

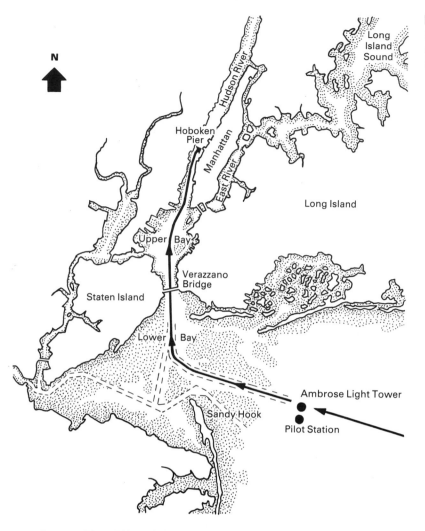

N

Long Island Sound

Hudson River

Hoboken Pier

Manhattan

East River

Long Island

Upper Bay

Verazzano Bridge

Staten Island

Lower Bay

Sandy Hook

Ambrose Light Tower

Pilot Station

heat and humidity of the New York late summer day on the morrow.

Having slept for several hours, the Master reappears in the Wheelhouse soon after 03.30hrs in response to the call from the First Officer on Watch. Bearing fine on the starboard bow is the strong flash of the Ambrose Light, and close to it the less distinct navigation lights of the cruising Pilot cutter which will be lowering its motor boat to transport the Pilot to the ship. When a mile or so from the Ambrose, the Master calls for a reduction of the engines to Combinator Mode, providing revolutions of 72 and propeller pitch to give about 6kt.

The appropriate parties have already been called to Arrival Stations in the same configuration as for arrival Cherbourg, the Carpenter and his mates unsecuring the anchors. The Second Officer on Watch now leaves the Bridge to supervise the opening of the shell door on No 5

Deck starboard and the lowering of the Pilot ladder, while the Master spots the lights of a big passenger ship approaching from the southeast, assuming it to be the Norwegian Wednesday arrival from Bermuda on its seven-day schedule and turnround. Had this been a Saturday, he could have expected a great procession of six or more cruise liners approaching on a similar course which, having boarded Pilots, would proceed up channel and into the harbour, as though jockeying for position to berth by 07.00hrs, the start of the working day for the shore gangs or longshoremen in local parlance.

At exactly 04.05hrs, with the ship edging up to Ambrose, the lights of the Pilot boat can be seen crossing her bow, to make a wide sweep on the starboard side and come up to the ladder. Powerful overside lights now play on the ladder as the boat approaches it, keeping pace with the momentum of the ship. Escorted by the Second

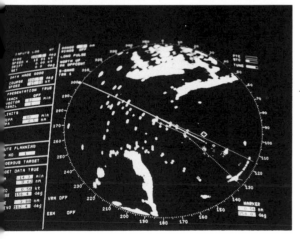

Officer on Watch, the New York Harbour – or Sandy Hook Pilot as he is sometimes named after the famous point of that name on the southern shore of the bay – arrives in the Wheelhouse.

'Good morning, Pilot,' the Master replies to his greeting, promptly informing him of the ship's course and speed – the latter having by this time built up to about 14kt on increased pitch. Now Master and pilot discuss whether conditions permit the higher revolution setting of 144 to be used. Both decide that they do, and by a combination of higher revs and pitch, the ship builds up to 18kt on a heading northwest up the Ambrose Channel. After covering some three miles, the Pilot calls 'Starboard twenty' and, about a mile later, another similar turn to bring the ship directly on a heading to the centre of the Narrows, so as to pass beneath the great Verazzano Bridge linking Brooklyn with Staten Island. Overhead a Jumbo Jet – hovering, as though suspended in space – its landing lights on and anti-collision beacon flashing, takes the lengthy Canarcy approach into JFK airport.

Far to the north there are repeated flickerings of lightning and the distant rumble of thunder. It is already oppressively hot and humid. Alive to the power of natural publicity the Master calls for the floodlighting to be switched on to give early commuters the thrill of seeing the great ship lit up, as she makes her stately procession towards the Verazzano. As she comes up with the spectacular, single-span structure, appearing as though her mast will hit it, the Pilot calls for reduced speed and the ship returns to about 14kt on 72 revolutions.

Lower New York Harbour, off Staten Island, is crowded as usual with anchored vessels: container ships, roll-on roll-off ferries and tankers, many of them awaiting orders – or berths – in Brooklyn, the East River, or tanker terminals on the Jersey shore bearing strange names like Perth Amboy or Marcus Hook. In such conditions it would be highly inappropriate to carry too much speed. With daylight comes the order 'Up Flags', whereupon the Assistant Coxswain on the Bridge runs up the Stars and Stripes to the masthead, the Blue Ensign to the gaff, pilot signal 'H' on one of the yardarms along with the houseflag and not forgetting the impressive 'Queen's Award' flag on the outer yard.

To the north a great mass of pitch black cloud, nearly constant lightning and now more audible peals of thunder pinpoint a summer storm raging over Long Island Sound and Connecticut. Now the decks beneath the Bridge are thronged with passengers – some of them the overnight revellers distinctly the worse for wear – all eager to witness one of the most beautiful harbour approaches in the world, many of them having watched it more times than they can count but anxious not to miss it again. Approaching to starboard are Governor's Island, and beyond it the entrance to the East River, dividing Manhattan from Brooklyn, while the stately Lady Liberty – refreshed by her recent facelift – dominates all else to port. There are unashamed cries of excitement from some of the younger newcomers standing on the promenade sun deck beneath the Wheelhouse.

The classic Manhattan skyline slowly unfolds ahead, dominated by the downtown World Trade Centre, its topmost storeys shrouded in swirling

Hoboken, New Jersey, to port. Here we see the familiar livery of a Moran tug – large white 'M' on an otherwise black stack – approaching from the Manhattan side. This is the tug of the Senior Master of the team, who doubles as the Docking Pilot in New York and will actually berth the ship. There are no people more experienced in the vagaries of the Hudson River than the New York tugmen, for whose skills the Cunard Masters' respect is boundless. Again the Second Officer on Watch has left the Bridge to meet the Pilot at the shell door on No 5 Deck starboard, while now the First Officer calls up the EnCR to ask for activation of the Bow Thrust.

The Dock Pilot arrives on the Bridge with a cheerful greeting to Master and Harbour Pilot, who tells him the ship's speed and course.

'Okay to take over Captain?' the Dock Pilot asks as a matter of courtesy.

'Go ahead, Pilot,' agrees the Master, after which the Moran skipper has the con in his dual role.

Now he calls for his additional tugs over his walkie-talkie, set to a particular frequency. There are usually three boats in attendance, but

Above:

Manhattan is shrouded in early morning haze as the River Pilot approaches by tug.

low cloud. Leaving the Battery to starboard, the *QE2* enters the Hudson River proper, or the North West as it is known locally, reducing speed to about 6kt. The big Norwegian liner has been content to take station on the port quarter, making no attempt to overtake on this occasion. The Pilot comments that she will be berthing at the pier across the slip from *QE2*.

QE2 is now approaching Pier 50 adjacent to West 14th Street on the starboard side and

Below left:
_QE2_ edges her way up the Hudson River.

Below:
'Driving Force 2' – from left to right: The New York River Pilot, Capt Alan Bennell, Senior First Officer Roy Hyde-Linaker and Staff Capt Ron Bolton.

sometimes four in trickier conditions – all named after members of the Moran family.

There is, perhaps, no more wayward stretch of water than the Hudson River off the Manhattan Piers for varying conditions, especially as the surface current of the river may frequently differ from the underwater flow to a significant extent. Not even the most experienced of the Moran skippers may know the extent of such variation from one moment to the next, and since the piers are positioned from shore at 90°, thrusting directly into the tideway, the ship must make a turn of that order to enter the slip and lay alongside – often a daunting manoeuvre. Today, however, conditions are such that the Dock Pilot deems three tugs to be sufficient and he positions one on the starboard bow forward and two on the same side aft. Unlike tugs at Southampton or Cherbourg, the New York boats do not make fast on a long towing wire. Instead they pass up their lines to mooring posts or bitts on the ship, in the aim of holding tight alongside in the best position to push against the hull at the appropriate moment.

The New York tugs are essentially pushers rather than pullers in the local berthing process and to the layman it is remarkable to witness the swiftness and the skill with which they can shift from one side of the ship to the other if called upon to do so. More remarkable, perhaps, is the method by which the tugs acknowledge the Pilot's successive orders – delivered to them over his walkie-talkie. They reply – not by the same method, but by whistle blast. However, the whistle in this case is not the tug's siren but something suggestive of a Walt Disney toyland locomotive in a well-practised code of short blasts. Given the chicanery of the Hudson tideway, there can be no uniform drill to berthing a ship at one of the piers.

Within the half-hour or so that the Dock Pilot takes the con to final mooring of the ship, it is not uncommon for him to issue upwards of 100 separate orders to tugs, main engines, rudder and Bow Thrust. To the onlooker the result seems akin to a bedlam of penny whistles, especially on summer Saturday mornings when perhaps five or six other cruise liners are berthing simultaneously at adjoining piers. But the fact remains that the system works – and very well at that!

The *QE2* has now come to a position across the slip, still heading upriver. Her intended berth is the upstream one, to which she will moor 'port side to'. By a combination of Bow Thrust to either side, rudder movement and propeller pitch – ahead or astern – the pilot holds her against wind and tide until satisfied that she is ready to make the turn of 90° into the slip. He achieves this – again by a combination of tugs pushing on the starboard side aft, engines (port ahead, starboard

Below:
The tug *Miriam Moran* makes fast on the starboard bow in preparation of the swing to starboard.

Above:
QE2 commences her turn . . .

Right, top to bottom:
. . . halfway there . . .

. . . easy does it!

Time to move ahead . . .

. . . not far to go now.

astern), thrust as needed and rudder hard to starboard. Today the operation is straightforward enough but it can be another matter when heavy rains up-state may swell the Hudson and increase current to a frightening extent in the form of so-called Freshets – sudden rushes of water – while in winter the added presence of ice on the tideway will give greater resistance to the ship's hull, making that much harder the task of the pushing tugs.

Once the ship is within the slip, however, it follows that the effect of tide will be considerably reduced – and wind likewise thanks to protection from the lofty piers. The final manoeuvre of placing the ship alongside thus becomes relatively straightforward at this point to the hardened expert, the three tugs now pushing on the starboard side and the Bow Thrust adding to momentum at the fore end. So as to achieve the required positioning against the pier, the Pilot must align the port wing of the Bridge with a vertical red-painted strake on the upper balcony of the terminal, but now he is also in touch with a colleague on the pierside, the Pier Foreman who must ensure that the entry ports in the ship's shell are exactly aligned with the shore gangway points and in no way obstructed by the terminal pillars.

Above:
With the first lines ashore it's just a question of lining her up on her marks.

Right:
Safely alongside and the first close-up view of New York is an almost empty car park!

With the light 'heaving-lines' having been successfully thrown ashore the forward mooring ropes have now been pulled to the quay and the eyes slipped over bollards by the longshoremen, while the same process follows aft as soon as the ship's stern is close enough for the heaving lines to be cast ashore. With the first lines on the pier, the Staff Captain gives the order 'Change Ensigns', at which the small Blue Ensign is run down from the gaff on the mast and replaced on the stern staff by its larger equivalent. In addition to the head and stern ropes – two at each end – backsprings are now passed out – one leading aft to the pier, the other forward. With all ropes tautened on tension, the mooring wires are now passed ashore – three forward, three aft including spring wires leading forward, and aft from the ship. All concerned are now moving swiftly, conscious that it is 07.15hrs and that the shore gangs are on pay, idly waiting to place the gangways and escalators in position.

Adjustment of the ship's position 5in astern is now called for by the Pier Foreman, and the Pilot tells the tugs to assist by angling their bows against the starboard hull facing half aft and steaming ahead to give a nudging effect. With the ship's position adjusted to exact requirements and the wires on tension, the Master calls for 'Finished with engines', and the machinery returns, after four days, to the Harbour Mode.

Both Pilots now take their leave and flag signal 'H' is run down, to be replaced immediately by 'P', the Blue Peter, denoting that the ship will sail later in the day for her return leg to Southampton. Arrival Stations are stood down, many of the men

to busy themselves through the day in preparation for the new voyage in but 8hr time – an unending cycle.

Having arrived in New York, the QE2 must disembark her passengers as speedily as possible. The first gangway to be positioned is the one leading to the main lobby on No 2 Deck amidships, by which the US Customs and other officialdom now board. Again in the interests of time-saving, given the ship's large passenger load, a pair of US Immigration Officers has accompanied the QE2 from Southampton, and has already checked passports as well as the appropriate entry form completed by each passenger. Thus at least one tiresome hurdle has been eliminated for people who have accepted that their experience is firmly over, and all they want now is to get ashore.

The Customs Officers are now escorted aft from the main lobby to the Purser's Office on the same deck, where the ship's documents are presented for their examination and approval. Following

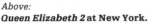

Above:
Queen Elizabeth 2 at New York.

Above right:
The 'Blue Peter' is hoisted, alongside the prestigious 'Queen's Award' flag, to denote that _QE2_ will sail within 24hr, homeward bound!

this they are taken to the Queen's Room, where the passengers wait patiently in line to have their Customs Declarations checked and approved (forms for which had been placed in cabins the previous day). Meanwhile all baggage which has been stacked in readiness for discharge is now rolling ashore on the escalators, to be set on the top level of the terminal according to colour tags tied to each piece by the bedroom stewards. However, no passenger is permitted ashore before the ship has been cleared finally of all

baggage – an irksome wait for many who cannot now help sensing that they have outstayed their welcome and that the ship's staff is only keyed up towards receiving its next load of human 'cargo'!

When finally they reach the terminal entrance to seek seemingly non-existent taxicabs and are struck by the hammer blow of New York heat and humidity, they wonder if the past few days have been anything more than a pleasant dream, glancing upwards to the _QE2's_ towering bow as though to assure themselves to the contrary.

At the escalator on No 5 Deck, storing has already commenced for the eastbound voyage and, on the starboard side, a bunkering tanker edges towards the ship to deliver fuel oil replenishment of some 1,600 tons.

Strangely, almost eerily, empty, the _Queen Elizabeth 2_ pauses for breath.